AND NOW, THE WEATHER...

AND NOW, THE WEATHER...

ALISON MALONEY

1 3 5 7 9 10 8 6 4 2

BBC Books, an imprint of Ebury Publishing
20 Vauxhall Bridge Road,
London SW1V 2SA

BBC Books is part of the Penguin Random House group of companies
whose addresses can be found at global.penguinrandomhouse.com

Copyright © Woodland Books Ltd 2017

First published by BBC Books in 2017

www.penguin.co.uk

ISBN 9781785942822

Author: Alison Maloney
Illustrations: Shutterstock

Typeset in India by Integra Software Services Pvt. Ltd, Pondicherry

Printed and bound in Great Britain by Clays Ltd, St Ives PLC

Penguin Random House is committed to a sustainable future for our
business, our readers and our planet. This book is made from Forest
Stewardship Council® certified paper.

Contents

Foreword by Carol Kirkwood

There are very few subjects covered in broadcasting that affect us all, and that we all have an opinion about. How many times a day do you find yourself talking about the weather – even just as a passing comment about how chilly it is? Will it be a hot summer? A white Christmas? I need rain for my garden! According to recent research, 94 per cent of British people admit to having discussed the weather in the past six hours, while 38 per cent say they have in the past 60 minutes. It certainly is a British obsession, and for many of us, BBC Weather is the place we go to for trusted forecasts and expert information.

My interest in weather started from a young age – not in the sense that I wanted to be a Weather Presenter – but rather that I grew up in the stunning northwest

Highlands of Scotland in a village called Morar, where we could literally have four seasons of weather in one day! This would, of course, dramatically alter the look of the landscape but more importantly to me in my youth, curtail my outdoor plans! In those days, weather forecasts were nowhere near as accessible as they are now, and we would have to wait until after the main news bulletins, and it was so annoying if you missed it! Nowadays, you can have weather forecasting on demand, for a wide range of locations in the UK and around the world. Never in my wildest dreams did I *ever* think I would one day be presenting the weather forecast that I so relied on as a child, on the BBC.

The way we present the weather today is different from when I started as a rookie. In those days it was quite formal. Today it is still presented professionally, but in a much chattier style, and often it is placed within a programme rather than as a standalone item at the end of the news, allowing some interaction with other presenters in a studio. Aside from being more fun, it also gives us the chance to explain big weather stories in the UK and around the world, why things are happening, or simply to explain what a jetstream is and its influence on our weather, or where you are likely to see the Aurora Borealis!

But probably one of the main changes is our weather graphics. Remember CEEFAX? We used to have to input that data onto a computer – it was so fiddly often East Anglia would end up as an island and it would be a nightmare trying to join it back onto the mainland again! In those days, when I joined the BBC Weather Centre back in the 1990s, our television graphics were still the sunshine and rain symbols (very 1970s!) not the magnetic ones I hasten to add, but the computer generated ones! We would drag and drop a symbol on the map, which was so big it would cover a whole area. So, for instance, the Midlands would a rain symbol for the entire morning, even if the rain was just for the early part of the morning and only affecting the west Midlands. The graphics would only change when the presenter clicked to move the charts onto the afternoon forecast. Of course it was the job of the presenter to explain all that. Then in 2005 the BBC introduced 3D graphics which completely changed the way we told the weather story. We now had graphics that moved around the UK to cover all areas, a clock that showed the time advancing through the day and night, and also moving weather elements – the cloud looked like cloud, and the rain like rain (albeit blue). This meant we could actually show what was happening where you were and what time you could expect the weather to change.

Now our graphics have changed once again, revolutionising the way we work. They look even more realistic and higher resolution data allow us to tell our audiences a more detailed story.

Of course one of the biggest changes over recent years has been the development of the BBC's digital weather services. I'm proud to say that the BBC Weather app is one of the most popular of all the BBC apps and delivers a great experience for people on the move or wanting to know the weather instantly. Personalisation has also been a key development in our digital services, so our users can get the local weather for their own postcode. With our most recent re-launch we have refreshed our weather website and app – with new functionality and detail.

New technology now helps me do my own job better too particularly when on location for BBC Breakfast. I used to have to rely on colleagues to brief me. Now I have access to much more online and can see and edit my charts from wherever I am in the UK.

I work with some of the brightest brains in meteorology. It is a pleasure to work with them all and discuss how we see the forecast evolving. We are always learning including from each other. Meteorology is not an exact science – but it is a fun one to study. The weather always changes and bigger brains than mine are constantly finding new ways to make forecasts even more accurate. I enjoy looking at what the weather is going to be way ahead of what we broadcast. Just like our audiences, we are keen to know if it is going to be dry and warm for our outdoor parties too – and we are as disappointed as anyone if the weather turns out to be different than expected! But there is very much a serious side to broadcasting a weather forecast. Sometimes knowing what is coming your way could even save your life and we work closely with the Met Office to ensure that any weather warnings are issued as quickly as possible.

Among the hundreds of weather broadcasts that I and my BBC colleagues do each day, one of the most treasured is the Shipping Forecast. It's a British institution in its own right these days – loved for its poetry and rhythm as well as being of utmost importance to people at sea for work or pleasure. The Shipping Forecast is one of a range of marine weather forecasts that is owned by the Maritime and Coastguard Agency and we partner with them to ensure that these are made available to the public.

So you see, it is not just you who talks about the weather – we do too! It is our passion and obsession.

I do hope you enjoy reading this book. You will learn there is a lot more to weather than you may have thought!

Carol

CHAPTER I

The History of the Weather Forecast

The weather is nothing new. Since time began, man has battled wind, rain, hail and snow and basked in glorious sunshine. But the ability to predict the weather has become an essential part of modern life for everyone from farmers, pilots and sailors to families planning a weekend and organisers of social events. So where did it all start?

ANCIENT WEATHERMEN

Man has been trying to master the art of forecasting the weather since civilisation began. The ancient Babylonians, in around 650 BC, used the appearance of clouds and other changes in the sky such as haloes around the sun and moon to predict what was to come, while the Chinese, circa 300 BC, attempted long-term predictions, creating a solar calendar which divided the year into twenty-four festivals, each associated with a different weather pattern. They also used the behaviour of wildlife to predict short-term weather. A cricket chirping at night, for example, indicated a fine day to come.

But it was the Ancient Greeks, and particularly Aristotle, who took weather forecasting to a whole new level. In 371 BC, Aristotle's pupil Theophrastus produced a book on weather forecasting called *The Book of Signs*. Thirty years later, in 340 BC, Aristotle wrote a four-volume tome called *Meteorologica*, which asserted that all things were made from four elements – fire, air, water and earth – and noted numerous observations on the weather. It described the cycle of water vapour rising from the earth under certain conditions in order to form clouds and ultimately rain, and detailed the formation of hurricanes, hail, snow and thunderstorms. For example, he wrote: 'Both dew and hoar-frost are found when the sky is clear and there is no wind. For the vapour could not be raised unless the sky were clear, and if a wind were blowing it could not condense.' On lightning, he observed, 'When there is a great quantity of exhalation and it is rare and is squeezed out in the cloud itself, we get a thunderbolt.'

The treatise closely linked changing conditions to astronomy and, although many of his theories would later be found to be inaccurate, it established Aristotle as the father of meteorology. In fact, it was not until the seventeenth century that many of his ideas were challenged and disproved.

The title of Aristotle's breakthrough work also explains why forecasting is known as meteorology. The word is derived from the Greek *meteoros*, meaning 'high up' or 'in the air', and *logia*, meaning to study and discuss. The Ancient Greek astronomers believed the weather was closely related to the stars and planets and that anything that came from the sky, including snow, hail, etc., was classed as a meteor.

The first instruments to help measure the weather began to appear in the fifteenth and sixteenth centuries. In 1480, Leonardo da Vinci built the first basic hygrometer, to measure the humidity of air, and in 1593 Italian physicist Galileo Galilei invented a thermoscope – the forerunner of the thermometer – after noticing that the density of a liquid changes in proportion to its temperature. Exactly fifty years later, his countryman Evangelista Torricelli invented the barometer to measure atmospheric pressure.

THE BEAUFORT SCALE

In 1805, Irish-born sailor Sir Francis Beaufort was serving on the HMS *Woolwich* when he devised a scale for measuring the strength of winds. Almost thirty years later, when he became the Royal Navy's Hydrographer – a scientist who studied properties of the ocean for navigational purposes – the scale was officially adopted and was first used on the HMS *Beagle*, under the command of Captain Robert FitzRoy, who went on to set up the first Meteorological Office.

The scale initially classed winds from 0 to 12. Rather than wind speed, Beaufort based the readings on the effect on the ship's sails running from 0 ('calm') and 1 ('just sufficient to give steerage') to 12 ('that which no canvas sails could withstand'). With the advent of steam power in the early twentieth century, the descriptions were changed from how the sails behaved to the sea itself. In 1923, Met Office Director George Simpson added the likely effect on land. The scale was extended to include forces 13 to 17 in 1946, but these were so rarely used that they were eventually dropped in most countries and the World Meteorological Organization's official scale only included 1–12. Only Taiwan and China, where typhoons are more common, still use the extended scale.

BEAUFORT'S ORIGINAL SCALE

Beaufort's 1831 Version of the Wind Scale			
0	Calm		
1	Light air	Or just sufficient to give steerage way	
2	Light breeze	Or that in which a man-of-war with all sail set and clean full would go in smooth water from –	1 to 2 knots
3	Gentle breeze		3 to 4 knots
4	Moderate breeze		4 to 5 knots
5	Fresh breeze	Or that in which a well-conditioned man-of-war could just carry, in chase, full and by –	Royals etc
6	Strong breeze		Single reefed topsails and top-gallant sails
7	Moderate gale		Double-reefed topsails, jib etc.
8	Fresh gale		Treble reefed topsails etc
9	Strong gale		Close reefed topsails and courses
10	Whole gale	Or that in which she could scarcely bear close reefed main topsail and reefed fore sail	
11	Storm	Or that which would reduce her to storm staysails	
12	Hurricane	Or that which no canvas could withstand	

THE BEAUFORT SCALE TODAY

**Current International Definitions on Sea and
on Land for the Beaufort Scale**

Force	Knots	Brief name	For use at sea	For use on land
0	< 1	Calm	Sea like a mirror.	Smoke rises vertically.
1	1–3	Light air	Ripples with the appearance of scales are formed, but without foam crests.	Direction of wind shown by smoke drift but not by wind vanes.
2	4–6	Light breeze	Small wavelets, still short but more pronounced. Crests have a glassy appearance and do not break.	Wind felt on face, leaves rustle, ordinary wind vanes moved by wind.
3	7–10	Gentle breeze	Large wavelets. Crests begin to break. Foam of glassy appearance. Perhaps scattered white horses.	Leaves and small twigs in constant motion, wind extends light flags.
4	11–16	Moderate breeze	Small waves, becoming longer, fairly frequent white horses.	Wind raises dust and loose paper, small branches move.
5	17–21	Fresh breeze	Moderate waves, taking a more pronounced form, many white horses are formed. Chance of some spray.	Small trees in leaf start to sway, crested wavelets on inland waters.
6	22–27	Strong breeze	Large waves begin to form, the white foam crests are more extensive everywhere. Probably some spray.	Large branches in motion, whistling in telegraph wires, umbrellas used with difficulty.
7	28–33	Near gale	Sea heaps up and white foam from breaking waves begins to be blown in streaks along the direction of the wind.	Whole trees in motion, inconvenient to walk against the wind.

Force	Knots	Brief name	For use at sea	For use on land
8	34–40	Gale	Moderately high waves of greater length; edges of crests begin to break into spindrift. The foam is blown in well-marked streaks along the direction of the wind.	Twigs break from trees, difficult to walk.
9	41–47	Strong gale	High waves. Dense streaks of foam along the direction of the wind. Crests of waves begin to topple, tumble and roll over. Spray may affect visibility.	Slight structural damage occurs, chimney pots and slates removed.
10	48–55	Storm	Very high waves with long over hanging crests. The resulting foam in great patches is blown in dense white streaks along the direction of the wind. On the whole, the surface of the sea takes on a white appearance. The 'tumbling' of the sea becomes heavy and shock-like. Visibility affected.	Trees uprooted, considerable structural damage occurs.
11	56–63	Violent storm	Exceptionally high waves (small and medium sized ships might be lost for a time behind the waves). The sea is completely covered with long white patches of foam lying along the direction of the wind. Everywhere, the edges of the waves are blown into froth. Visibility affected.	Widespread damage.
12	64	Hurricane	The air is filled with foam and spray. Sea completely white with driving spray, visibility very seriously affected.	Widespread damage.

SPREADING THE WORD

While instruments for measuring and recording weather were refined throughout the seventeenth and eighteenth centuries, it was the invention of the telegraph in the mid-nineteenth century which opened up a network for weather observers and data collectors to communicate – and the creation of the first weather maps.

The Smithsonian Institution got the ball rolling in 1849 by supplying weather instruments to telegraph companies, who found 150 volunteers across the USA to take readings which were then fed back allowing the Smithsonian to map out wind and storm patterns. Soon weather observation stations began springing up all over the world and the information shared saw the birth of synoptic weather forecasting, meaning the data was recorded at intervals of six hours.

THE ROYAL METEOROLOGICAL SOCIETY

The British Meteorological Society was formed in 1850 by a group of ten astronomers and meteorologists in order to promote the 'advancement and extension of meteorological science by determining the laws of climate and of meteorological phenomena in general'. In 1866, it was incorporated into the Royal Charter, and in 1883 it became the Royal Meteorological Society when Queen Victoria granted them the use of the prefix.

One of its founding members, James Glaisher, was a pioneering balloonist as well as an eminent astronomer at the Royal Observatory, Greenwich. Between 1862 and 1866, he made frequent balloon flights to measure the temperature and humidity of the atmosphere at its highest levels. On one ascent in 1862, he broke the world record for altitude, rising to an estimated seven miles above sea level. Unfortunately, due to the thin air at such an altitude, he passed out before he could take any readings and the pigeon he was carrying on board died.

In 1921, the group merged with the Scottish Meteorological Society, set up in 1855 by David Milne-Home and privately funded by landowners with a vested interest in advance weather warnings.

THE MET OFFICE

In 1854, despite advances in reading the atmospheric signs of weather, many still believed it could not be forecast. When one forward-thinking MP suggested to the House of Commons that they would soon be able to tell what the weather would be like in London, twenty-four hours ahead, he was met with roars of laughter.

Nonetheless, a small department called the Meteorological Office was set up within the Board of Trade that same year. Under the leadership of naval officer Captain Robert FitzRoy, the new section aimed to offer advice on likely weather events to the whole marine community. In the five years to come, 7,201 lives would be lost at sea and Captain FitzRoy believed many of those could have been saved if better weather warnings were in place.

In 1859, a tragedy that overshadowed all previous disasters struck on the high seas when a passenger ship, the *Royal Charter*, was caught in a huge storm measuring 12 on the Beaufort Scale. The ship – carrying 312 passengers, 112 crew and a few company employees – was returning to Liverpool from Melbourne when the high winds of over 100 mph smashed it against the rocks off the coast of Anglesey. Around 450 lives were lost, and only 21 passengers and 18 crew members survived.

In the wake of the terrible tragedy, Robert FitzRoy introduced a system of gale warnings which were issued to mariners whenever a storm was expected. He established eighteen weather stations around the coast, which used barometers and other instruments to gauge the weather and reported back to the Met Office by telegraph. FitzRoy would then study the reading and, if he thought a storm was imminent, he would telegraph a warning back.

A visual system of cones and drums, hoisted onto a 40-foot mast in the harbour, was then used to signal the sea conditions to the ships during the day, and lights after dark. For example, a cone pointing upwards indicated a gale from the north and pointing downwards, from the south. A lone drum signalled stormy weather, and a drum with a cone indicated a storm from the direction indicated. At night, three lights forming a triangle replaced the cones and four lights in a square, the drum.

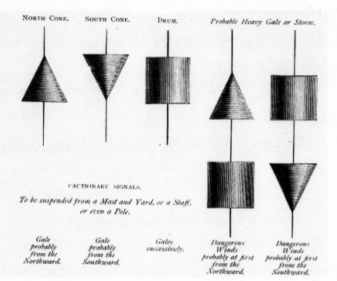

'Daytime Storm Signal' from *The Weather Book: A Manual of Practical Meteorology* by Rear Admiral Robert FitzRoy (1863). Courtesy NOAA Treasures of the NOAA Library Collection, US Dept of Commerce.

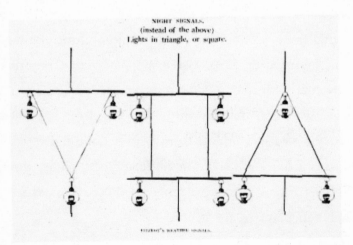

'Night Storm Signal' from *The Weather Book : A Manual of Practical Meteorology* by Rear Admiral Robert FitzRoy (1863). Courtesy NOAA Treasures of the NOAA Library Collection, US Dept of Commerce.

The Times weather forecast for 1 August 1861, the first to appear in print, was produced under the heading 'General weather probable during the next two days'. It came in the form of a table, charting barometer readings, temperature, wind speed, wind force and sea disturbance. One column also detailed the conditions with an initial, e.g. 'b' for blue sky, 'c' for cloud, 'l' for lightning, 'h' for hail, 'r' for rain and 's' for snow.

The first forecast predicted London would be 62F, clear with a south-westerly wind, Liverpool would be 61F, very cloudy with a light south-westerly wind and Portsmouth and Penzance were set to be overcast, with temperatures around 61F. Dover was enjoying some especially warm weather with the thermometer predicted to hit 70F.

To help those heading to sea, predictions weren't confined to the UK but also included Lisbon, Copenhagen, Brest, Bayonne and Helder.

The more general round-up at the bottom read:

North – Moderate westerly wind; fine.

> *West – Moderate south-westerly; fine.*
>
> *South – Fresh westerly; fine.*
>
> East was omitted from the first forecasts but was added a few days later.

A year after the weather warnings began to be signalled to ships, Admiral FitzRoy's first daily forecast was printed in *The Times*.

The first forecasts were surprisingly accurate and were greeted, on the whole, with high praise and wonder. A journalist in Dublin's *Freeman's Journal* wrote: 'Persons have been astonished by the weather predictions of Admiral FitzRoy. They have been in the main most accurate, particularly in the direction of air currents.'

One paper, the *Morning Post*, bemoaned the passing of the more traditional folklore, saying: 'The old adage "As uncertain as the winds" had ceased, we are told, to be a correct comparison, for the winds are said to be governed by fixed laws. To call a man "a weathercock" is no longer a term of reproach.'

Thanks to the coastal warnings and the daily print projections, the number of shipwrecks around the UK dropped and, for the most part, Admiral FitzRoy's forecasts were a popular innovation. But the government was beginning to make noises about the cost of the operation, some scientists claimed the mariner turned meteorologist had no solid theory on which to base his predictions, and the press could not resist the occasional dig when FitzRoy got it wrong.

After one bad run, the *Bath Chronicle* commented: 'Ever since Admiral FitzRoy took to telling us what to look for, the weather seems to have felt insulted, and to act as capriciously as a wit, who is asked out to dinner to amuse people, and revenges himself by alterations of dullness and petulance.'

After FitzRoy's death in 1865, the work of the Meteorological Office came under scrutiny from the accountants at the Board of Trade, who believed the forecasts were not sufficient value for money. A Royal Society inquiry concluded that the storm warnings were 'of some use' but advised that the daily forecasts should be dropped. The last one was published in *The Times* on 28 March 1866, and weather maps did not return to the papers until 1879.

ROBERT FITZROY – THE FIRST ADMIRAL OF THE BLEW

Admiral FitzRoy was 54 when his weather forecasts made him a national talking point – *Punch* even dubbed him First Admiral of the Blew – but he already had an illustrious career behind him and had found fame as the captain of Charles Darwin's ship, HMS *Beagle*.

Robert FitzRoy was born into an aristocratic family in Surrey, the fourth great grandson of Charles II, on 5 July 1805. The son of General Lord Charles FitzRoy, a British Army Officer and aide-de-camp to George III, and his second wife Lady Frances Stewart, Robert FitzRoy was raised at Wakefield Lodge, in Northamptonshire. In 1818, at the age of 12, he was sent to the Royal Naval College in Portsmouth. Two years later, he was already on the high seas, embarking on a two-year voyage to South America on the frigate HMS *Owen Glendower* as a voluntary student and being promoted to midshipman while at sea.

After completing his naval course, and becoming the first student to get 100 per cent in his exams, he was appointed flag lieutenant on the HMS *Ganges* before joining HMS *Beagle* in 1828, when it was part of a scientific expedition to South America. When the captain,

Pringle Stokes, shot himself, FitzRoy took his place and by the time he returned to Britain, in October 1830, he had established his reputation as a fine commander and surveyor. He also brought back four native children, captured during an attempt to steal the *Beagle*, who he planned to convert to Christianity and 'civilise'. One died and the other three were taken in by missionary Richard Matthews, and were considered civilised enough to present to the court of King William IV and Queen Adelaide a year later.

Determined HMS *Beagle* would sail again, FitzRoy struggled to raise the finances until his uncle, the Duke of Grafton, put pressure on the Admiralty and, in June 1831, he was reappointed as the ship's captain. He asked his friend Beaufort, who was to sail with him, to find a male companion whose company he would enjoy and who would make the most of the natural history opportunities on the voyage. That man was to be Charles Darwin, who would later use his findings from the trip for *The Origin of Species*.

During the expedition, which covered the Falkland Islands, Chile, Galapagos, Tahiti, New Zealand, Australia, South Africa and Brazil, the pair became firm friends, although FitzRoy's explosive temper did lead to some arguments, most notably a humdinger over the rights and wrongs of slavery which saw Darwin banished from the Captain's table.

Although he embraced the ideas of Darwin and his predecessor Charles Lyell at the time, he was conflicted because of his firm belief in the Bible. In his account of the voyage, published in 1839, he admitted his head had been turned by 'geologists who contradict, by implication, if not in plain terms, the authenticity of the Scriptures' but said that, after renewing his acquaintance with the Good Book, he believed in the six-day creation and that seashells spotted high in rock mountains were evidence of Noah's Flood.

Years later, in 1860, FitzRoy denounced Darwin's historic publication at a public meeting in Oxford. Holding a copy of the Bible, he stood up in the audience and begged those present to 'believe God rather than man', admitting *The Origin of Species* had given him 'acutest pain'.

On his return to shore, FitzRoy married Mary Henrietta O'Brien, with whom he would have four children. In 1837, he was also awarded a gold medal by the Royal Geographical Society for his work on HMS *Beagle*, and five years later he was elected as Tory MP for Durham. After a short and unsuccessful stint as the Governor of New Zealand, FitzRoy briefly returned to sea before retiring from his naval career in 1850, at the age of 45.

FitzRoy was put forward for the post at the Board of Trade, setting up what would become the Met Office, by his former shipmate Beaufort and he proved the perfect candidate. Passionate about the perils of those at sea, he worked hard to make his warnings as accurate as possible and he was proud of his work. After *The Times* congratulated him for the first ever gale warning, on 6 February 1861, he wrote a letter back boasting that 'the event was predicted with as much certainty as an eclipse and could have been announced with signals as conspicuous as fiery beacons'.

The expansion of his forecasts to the newspaper meant that not only sailors benefitted from his meticulous calculation, but organisers of events like church fetes, horse races, sporting events and many more could take advantage of prior knowledge of likely conditions. He even had a royal fan – Queen Victoria once sent her aides to his home to ask if the sea would be calm for her crossing to the Isle of Wight, where she planned a stay at the Royal residence Osborne House.

However, not everyone was thrilled with his forecasts. In fact some were irritated when he predicted bad weather, as if he had brought it on, and owners of fishing fleets were not happy when his warnings meant the fishermen refused to go out for the whole day. There were also occasions when the predictions proved wildly wrong, and FitzRoy was happy to hold his hands up, addressing a letter in the paper, on one occasion, to 'those whose hats have been spoilt from umbrellas being omitted'.

Even though his weather experiment had largely proved a success, however, it didn't prevent the black clouds forming in his personal life. By 1865, now married to his second wife Maria and bringing up his fifth child, Robert FitzRoy succumbed to crippling depression. He moved from London to Norwood in search of fresh air but was unable to get out of bed most days, let alone work.

On Sunday 30 April 1865, the 59-year-old got up to get dressed and ready for church, as usual, and kissed his youngest daughter, Laura Elizabeth, before going into his dressing room, locking the door and cutting his own throat.

It later came to light that the entire family fortune of £6,000 (the equivalent of £500,000 today) had been used as public expenditure. Friends and campaigners eventually persuaded the government to repay £3,000 to his widow and Queen Victoria, moved by their plight, allowed Maria and Laura Elizabeth to move into a grace-and-favour flat.

Vice-Admiral FitzRoy is buried in the churchyard at All Saints' Church in Upper Norwood, South London and the Met Office now resides in a street in Exeter named FitzRoy Road, in tribute to their founder.

BUCHAN SPELLS

As Admiral FitzRoy was busy perfecting his storm warning for mariners, another eminent meteorologist was making waves north of the border. Alexander Buchan had started his career as a teacher, studying meteorology in his spare time, but when he lost his voice and was forced to retire from the classroom, he turned his attentions to his true passions. As the secretary of the Scottish Meteorological Society from 1860 until his death from pneumonia in 1907 at the age of 78, he made great strides in the science and was the brains behind the modern weather map.

In the 1860s, Buchan began to put data on sea-level pressure onto charts and then join the points of equal pressure using lines – now familiar to weather watchers as isobars. In this way he was able to plot the movement of high-pressure and low-pressure fronts and come up with a long-term forecast.

In 1863, Buchan created a series of eighteen charts detailing the development and movement of weather systems across Europe and plotting wind speed and direction. From these he was able to deduce that winds blow anti-clockwise around an area of low pressure in the Northern Hemisphere, and that wind speed is proportionate to the closeness of the isobars, i.e. the barometric gradient.

His 1868 book, *The Handy Book of Meteorology*, was the first to make long-range weather predictions. It also noted the dates in the year when anomalies in temperature are likely to occur, which are now known as 'Buchan spells'. For example, a cold Buchan spell typically occurs just before Valentine's Day and again in the first week of April, often bringing a late frost. There are also warm Buchan spells in the second week of July, another in August and one in the first week of December.

SPREADING THE WORD

Soon after FitzRoy's death, the USA followed his lead and, in 1870, a resolution passed by President Ulysses S. Grant established the National Weather Service. Its purpose, he declared, was 'to provide for taking meteorological observations at the military stations in the interior of the continent and at other points in the States and Territories … and for giving notice on the northern (Great) Lakes and on the seacoast by magnetic telegraph and marine signals, of the approach and force of storms'.

As it was decided that the military would have the necessary skills to carry out the task with precision and efficiency, the new service was put under the umbrella of the Department of War who in turn assigned the task to the Signal Service Corps under Brigadier General Albert J. Myer. Meteorological readings were taken at the military bases and other points around the country and the forecasts began to be regularly issued later the same year.

In 1890, forecasting was switched to the Department of Agriculture and the United States Weather Bureau was born, although it was later to revert to its original name, the National Weather Service.

FROM FORECAST TO BROADCAST

The advent of radio and, later, television led to the weather forecast becoming an everyday part of modern life. In Britain, the first radio forecasts, including gale and storm warnings, were issued by the Met Office to ships and coastguards in 1911, although they were suspended during the First World War. In 1922, the BBC began broadcasting the Shipping Forecast on behalf of the Met Office and a year later the first daily forecasts began. The USA followed suit in 1925, with their first radio forecast, produced in Boston by Edward B. Rideout.

The first weather maps to be televised, in 1936, filled the screen and the announcer could be heard off screen, running through conditions for the next few days. But the BBC was off air during the Second World War, and the maps didn't make a comeback until 1949.

Five years later, the modern-day weather presenter was born when George Cowling stood in front of the map and pointed at the relevant areas on camera in a slot lasting five minutes, rather than the previous few seconds. The *Radio Times* announced: 'From Monday onwards the television weather report and forecast will be presented by a Meteorological Office forecaster who will explain and comment on the charts shown. The change is designed to stress the continuity of the reports provided; the forecaster will show, for example, how the weather expected tomorrow is conditioned by the weather experienced today.'

The London Weather Centre, set up by the Met Office in 1959, provided a point of contact for members of the public and businesses and a chance to see the meteorologists at work. It also provided the weather presenters, who were auditioned by the BBC before going on air. It was the first of thirteen centres that were to spring up around the country, eventually leading to a more regional approach to forecasting.

At the birth of the TV forecast, maps were hand drawn by the presenter and couriered across London, and they were not always accurate. The first computer, in 1962, improved matters slightly, but it was not until 1973 that a high-tech update at the Weather Centre allowed the BBC to use satellite imagery, which had been around for nearly a decade but was of such poor quality that, up until that point, the coastline had to be drawn in with felt-tip pens.

Technological advances saw the hand-drawn signs replaced with magnetic symbols, which could be stuck onto the map of the UK and easily moved as weather fronts advanced, but they had a tendency to drop off and could all too easily be put on upside down or in the wrong place. They were replaced by computer graphics in 1985 and, at the turn of the century, new symbols representing the pollen count and sun levels were added. BBC weather also became available online in 1997 and in 2013, the first smartphone app was launched.

In the USA, television forecasts were first brought to the screen in Cincinnati in the 1940s, on the DuMont Television Network. In the late 1970s, *Good Morning America*'s John Coleman, one of the first 'celebrity' weathermen, pioneered the use of satellite and computer-generated images on TV, and in 1982 he set up *The Weather Channel*, the first 24-hour network devoted entirely to forecasting.

Brits are obsessed with the weather, perhaps because our weather is so changeable. It's rare that we get any lengthy spell of significant weather. Also, I think it goes back to the war when forecasting the weather was so important.

The forecasters had a really stressful job back then without the use of computers and satellite imagery and their forecasts were literally a matter of life and death for anyone on the sea, for example for the D-Day landings.

Louise Lear, weather presenter

RADAR

A breakthrough in technology designed to detect enemy aircraft during the Second World War also provided a boon to early weather forecasting. Robert Watson-Watt, a meteorologist by training, patented the first radar system in 1935. Although he was interested in its uses to detect thunderstorms, war with Germany was on the horizon, so Watson-Watt turned his attention to its use to airmen in detecting the whereabouts of incoming aircraft.

Despite there being more pressing uses for radar during the Second World War, the Met Office did set up its first radar research centre in East Hill, Bedfordshire, initially concentrating on turbulence and cloud activity. In the early 1950s, scientists began to use radar echoes to determine the nature of thunderstorms and lightning and to measure the accuracy of rainfall forecasts and, in 1955, a radar was installed in London for the use of the Met Office forecasters.

At the same time, the use of the Doppler Weather Radar was being adopted in the US in a bid to predict the strength and likely paths of tornadoes. As technology advanced, radar became an essential tool in weather prediction and, from the 1980s, a huge network of radars was built across the USA and Canada, as well as in Britain. Today, radar is still used widely and investigations have found the radar readings more accurate than those taken from a network of rain gauges.

There are currently eighteen weather radars in the UK, ranging from Drum-A-Starraig in the north to Predannack in Cornwall to the south.

EYES IN THE SKY

On 1 April 1960, the USA made a huge breakthrough in weather observation when the first polar-orbiting satellite TIROS-1 (Television and Infrared Observation Satellite) was launched into space. The weather satellite was the culmination of years of work by the National Aeronautics and Space Administration (NASA) in partnership with the United States Army, Radio Corporation of America, the US Weather Bureau, the United States Naval Photographic Interpretation Center (NPIC), the Environmental Science Services Administration (ESSA), and the National Oceanic and Atmospheric Administration (NOAA).

Shaped like a drum, the 122 kg instrument was 1.1 m in diameter and 48 cm high and was mounted with two slow-scan cameras, which took half a second to record each image. Sent into orbit by a Thor Able space rocket, the satellite stabilised by spinning at 135 rpm, but as soon as it locked into orbit it slowed to 12 rpm, to enable clear photos to be taken. The images gathered were sent back to NASA via FM transmitters and, as soon as they were received, the tape wiped itself clean and started filming again.

Although the TIROS-1 suffered a catastrophic failure after 78 days, it did capture pictures of the Earth from space which proved useful for scientists and it also paved the way for nine more TIROS satellites to follow. In 1966, the model gave way to more advanced versions, known as the Tiros-N and NOAA satellites which continue to send weather pictures to Earth today. Nine of the original TIROS devices are still in space.

A second type of satellite, geostationary, was launched by Japanese scientists in 1977. Unlike the orbiting instruments, the Himawari was designed to orbit the Earth above the equator at an altitude of 35,880 km (22,300 miles). As the Earth turns, the geostationary satellite stays with it, recording and transmitting the hemisphere below from the same spot. The USA and Russia have since put geostationary satellites into orbit and it is these images that are used in modern-day weather reports, as they show cloud and weather fronts shifting over the same spot rather than moving across the Earth.

CHAPTER 2

Amateur Hour

It's not just those clever people at the Met Office who know when the next heatwave is coming and whether it's time to batten down the hatches against a storm. Mother Nature has a fair inkling, and there is an army of amateur forecasters who take her hints very seriously. Whether it's the birds and the bees or the size of fruit blossom, there are a myriad of natural clues in gardens and hedgerows everywhere.

One weather specialist, David King, has spent years collecting tried and tested methods of predicting the weather using the world around him. He gathered information from over 800 farmers and thatchers and has now whittled them down to a fool-proof arsenal of forecasting tools which, he claims, give him an impressive average accuracy of 90 per cent.

'Occasionally I even hit 100 per cent, and get everything completely right,' says David. 'And that's great, proving that the old ways can beat the technology of the day – much to the chagrin of experts.'

Former policeman David grew up in Devon, surrounded by countryside, and learned about his natural habitat as a boy. 'I grew up on the edge of Dartmoor, and there was no TV in those days,' he says. 'We went out hunting with ferrets and running about on the moor and we got to know nature so well. My uncles would tell me how to read the signs from nature.'

During his career in the Metropolitan Police he started to develop an interest in climatology. 'I worked beside the Thames, and in those days London was one of the biggest ports in the world, so the big coal barges and ships would come up the river. I watched the river and saw how the tides affected everything.'

He also learned a thing or two about the stars and the moon, from an old Second World War fighter pilot, and started to research ancient methods of weather prediction. 'Some clever monks worked out how to predict the weather using moon cycles a thousand years ago and wrote it all down,' he revealed. 'They divided the day into two-hour segments and discovered if you can work out the phase of the moon in each segment, you can predict the weather. Using this method, I work out the weather up to two years ahead and I will guarantee a minimum of 90 per cent accuracy.'

He also swears by some weather 'rules' that have come from studying patterns throughout history:

☀ *There are four 'quarter days' in the year. They are 21 March, 24 June, 29 September and 21 December. The direction the wind blows on each of these days is the predominant direction it will blow for the next 90 days.*

☀ *Every fifteen years, we get a really bad winter. We had one in 1976, 1991 and 2002, so add another fifteen years and that takes you to 2017.*

☀ *There are always storms just after Christmas Day, so Boxing Day to New Year's Eve are likely to be blustery.*

Here are some of David's top tips for forecasting the weather.

1. Taller flowers mean more rain

If the weather is going to be wet, plants that produce seeds that are staple foods for birds, such as giant hogweed, thistles, burdock and teasel, raise themselves away from the damp ground and grow taller, making them easier pickings for hungry birds.

2. Fewer bird chicks means a rotten summer

If blackbirds and tits have one brood in the spring, rather than two, it's likely to be a worse summer than usual.

3. Early migration means an early autumn

If the swallows, martins and cuckoos have flown before the end of August, it's time to put the barbecue away and stack up the sun loungers. There won't be any more hot days coming your way.

4. Late nesting means a late summer

Birds such as tits and house martins can start building nests as early as March. If they are still not nesting by May, summer will be late in coming.

5. If the birds are fat, keep your winter coat to hand

Look at the blackbirds and robins in February and March; if they are plump, there is more frosty weather to come. Birds store fat to see them through the cold spells.

6. Look for the lily pads

An abundance of lily pads on the river, in the late spring, is a sure sign that summer is on the way. And when you see the dragonflies buzzing around, reach for the sunscreen.

7. Blackberries tell us how long summer will last

If blackberry bushes haven't blossomed by the end of May, we are in for a late start to summer. The good news is that it is likely to last longer into the traditional autumn months.

8. Know your onions

Slice into an onion in the late autumn, early winter. If it has a thicker skin than normal, we're in for a cold, hard winter.

9. Woolly winter forecast

If you have a field of sheep nearby, take a look at their wool in November. If it is fuller and thicker than usual, it will be a long, harsh winter.

10. Nutty nature

If squirrels are hiding nuts in the tree, it is going to be a cold winter. Although people assume squirrels dig and bury their stores, if it's going to be cold and the ground is likely to freeze, they keep them above ground. Jays, which also bury food for winter, will hide it in a tree on the approach to a bad winter. If the ground freezes over, their beaks won't be able to break through so they have to keep it somewhere more accessible.

FOGGITT'S FORECASTS

Among the most famous of the amateur weather forecasters was Bill Foggitt, whose slot on Yorkshire Television during the 1980s was legendary. Using the behaviour of moles, snails and flowers in his hometown of Thirsk, Bill predicted upcoming conditions with incredible accuracy.

For Bill, who died in 2004 at the age of 91, climatology was in the blood. Although the Foggitt family ran successful pharmacies in Thirsk for 200 years, generation after generation also had a passion for forecasting, passed down through weather diaries they kept as a family tradition. They were started by Bill's great-great-great grandfather in 1771, inspired by a devastating flood which swept through the nearby town of Yarm, destroying homes and shops, damaging the church and killing nine people. The theory was that if he studied the weather he could help predict future disasters so local people were prepared.

Through his observations, he developed an understanding of cyclical weather and identified a pattern of outstanding summers recurring every twenty-two years and severe winters every fifteen. He became a well-respected climatologist and a member of the Linnean Society, a biological fellowship set up in 1788.

Two centuries later, his descendant Bill became a local celebrity by using the homespun weather theories, and his knowledge of nature, to predict the weather. He first came to the attention of the media in 1946, when he wrote to a newspaper to warn that a flock of waxwings, seen out of season in Thirsk, meant a cold winter was coming. He was soon asked to write a column in the *Yorkshire Post*, which was named Foggitt's Forecast. But it wasn't until 1985 that TV fame came calling, after he disagreed with the Met Office prediction of a prolonged Arctic snap, writing: 'I don't think so. I have noticed a mole poking its nose through the snow and that invariably means warmer weather is on its way.' When the warmer weather duly arrived, so did journalists from around the country and Bill landed his TV slot.

He was snapped up for a regular slot by Yorkshire Television. In his charming forecasts, he would tell viewers it was about to rain because the pine cones had closed up, or the seaweed in the local bay had become slimy, and would regale them with tales of mole behaviour, sheep acting out of sorts and bird habits plus observation such as the fact that flies behaved sluggishly before thunderstorms. His natural weather methods were greatly respected, and the Association of Science Education even included his work in a textbook for schools. In the summer of 1985, he beat Michael Fish in a forecasting face-off in the *Yorkshire Post*, achieving an accuracy rating of 88 per cent, as opposed to Michael's 74 per cent.

WEATHER WATCHERS

In November 2015, the BBC launched Weather Watchers, a crowd-sourcing forum which invites enthusiasts to share photos and reports from their own location, and there has been a huge response

Liz Howell, Head of BBC Weather said: 'When we planned this as part of our Make It Digital project we expected to get about 50,000 weather watchers joining our club, but we have nearly 160,000 and growing! They have posted more than 1.4 million reports to date.'

The BBC, with help from their partners at the Royal Meteorological Society, are able to gauge everything from snow and storms to blazing sunshine across the UK, the moment it arrives.

Liz adds: 'Weather Watchers have become a real part of our broadcasting and storytelling. They are a fabulous bunch of people and we love having them as our roving reporters!'

Many of the stunning pictures taken by the watchers are used every day as backdrops to the TV weather forecasts.

'Weather Watchers includes our viewers directly in our broadcasts and help us show off our green and pleasant land, coastlines and cities,' says Carol Kirkwood.

'Before we would illustrate contrasts in the weather using a satellite picture. Now we have a choice or we can use both. Our weather watchers have become an invaluable and much loved part of the BBC weather family.'

WEATHER WISE

With the internet, social media and smartphone apps readily available, it has never been easier to indulge a passion for the weather and there are many tools that amateur enthusiasts can reach for.

As well as BBC Weather Watchers and the Met Office's Weather Observation Website, WOW, many use Weather Underground, or Wunderground for short, or join the Climatological Observers Link and TORRO, run by the Tornado and Storm Research Organisation. The Weather Club, run by the Royal Meteorological Society (RMetS), is an online community which allows people to access information and share views online and many also join the society, which now has over 1000 amateur meteorologists amongst its members.

Professor Liz Bentley, Chief Executive of the RMets, said: 'The Royal Meteorological Society is a charity that supports the meteorological community, whether that is weather service providers or users of weather information, scientists, forecasters, teachers, students or those who simply have an interest in weather and climate.'

As such the society hosts around 75 meetings and conferences across the UK, each year, where those in the community can share their knowledge of the science and applications of meteorology. They also publish seven international journals, including the monthly magazine, Weather, which readers can view in print, online or via an app.

For professionals, the RMets provides accreditation, such as the Chartered Meteorologist, and they also provide educational resources for teachers and clubs to boost interest in the weather and the climate and encourage young people to get involved.

Professor Bentley adds: 'The RMetS was actively involved in the last review of the National Curriculum to ensure that weather and climate was embedded in the core curriculum for A Level Geography.'

CHAPTER 3
Lost in Translation

Brits love nothing more than talking about the weather, and barely a chance meeting in the street goes by without a quick summary of current conditions. But while the whole country has much the same weather, at different times and to varying degrees, the way we describe it differs from region to region. While a Scot may tell you it's 'dreich' outside, a Devonian will moan about the 'mizzle', and a Yorkshireman may fret about the 'fret'.

So dig out your sou'westers for a blustery tour of the UK's colloquial weather words.

Airish Mainly heard in Scotland, airish means cool, fresh, breezy and chilly.

Barber A severe snow or sleet storm at sea, during freezing weather.

Blackthorn winter From the South East of England, this describes cold winds in the Thames Valley during March and April.

Cat's nose In England, a cool north-west wind.

Caver (or kaver) A gentle breeze in the Hebridean islands, in the west of Scotland.

Cortilly weather A Cornish term meaning foggy or misty.

Cow-quaker A traditional and wonderfully descriptive term for a sudden, heavy rainstorm in May, after the cows have returned to the fields from wintering indoors. Pummelled by the cold rains, the cows would huddle together shivering in the rain and wind.

Custard winds A curious term for cold easterly winds, from the northeast coast of England. The origin is unknown but one theory is that the winds blow around Easter, when folk traditionally tucked into puddings and custard in the post-Lent feasts.

Dimpsey A descriptive West Country word meaning dull, damp and drizzly.

Dreich The Scottish word for damp, dreary, gloomy weather is pronounced 'dree-ch' with the 'ch' similar to that of 'loch'. In 2013, 'dreich' was named as the Scots' favourite regional word in a YouGov poll, with 23 per cent of the vote.

Drookit From Scotland, meaning drenched or soaked through by rain.

Dryth This Welsh and West Country saying is quite self-explanatory, meaning drought or dry spell.

Farmer's year Used in many rural areas, meaning the 12-month period starting with the Sunday nearest to 1 March.

Fen blow A wind blowing dust over farming land during a dry spell, specifically in East Anglia.

Flanders storm In England, a heavy fall of snow coming with the south wind.

Flist A sudden shower and squally storm in Scotland.

Fowan A dry, scorching wind on the Isle of Man.

Fret In Yorkshire and Northumberland, they call a sea fog a 'fret' or 'sea fret'.

Gosling blast A sudden squall of rain or sleet in England.

Gowk storm Derived from *gouk*, the Nordic word for cuckoo, gowk has also come to mean 'fool' in Scotland. The gowk storm is an unseasonal storm or snow storm which happens in April, close to April Fool's Day and at a time when the cuckoo would usually be heralding the arrival of spring.

Haar The cold sea fog that rolls in from the northeast coast of England on the North Sea in Scotland.

Hooring More innocent than it sounds, this is an Irish term for absolutely chucking it down.

Hurly-burly A fierce thunderstorm with high winds, usually in the south east.

Lamb blast or Lambing storm A late snowstorm in the spring, as the lambs are being born.

Letty In Somerset, this refers to weather such as heavy rain and winds that hinders or 'lets' work that needs to be done outside.

MANANNAN'S CLOAK

A thick impenetrable sea-fog that envelops the Isle of Man. Manannan, the God of the Sea from many Celtic myths, is also known as the protector of the island and the deity who put the 'Man' into its name. Legend has it that when unwanted visitors or enemies approach the isle, he throws a cloak of thick mist over it to hide it from view and keep it safe. The grey fog, which rolls in from the water, then shrouds the island from enemy eyes until they have passed.

Maumy It may not sound like it, but 'Maumy' is a good thing. The word, from northern England, means mellow weather, soft and mild.

Mizzle A word combined from 'mist' and 'drizzle' meaning exactly that – very fine rain. Used in Devon, Cornwall and Northumberland.

Mochy Scottish and Irish, meaning damp, moist and muggy.

Mothery This one has nothing to do with maternal smothering. It's a Lincolnshire term meaning damp and drizzly.

Naysh Devon term meaning cold.

Northern Nanny A southern phrase for a freezing cold storm coming down from the north.

Pitch Snow that sticks to the ground in the West Country.

Plash From Northumberland, meaning a heavy and sudden downpour of rain.

Robin Hood wind The name given to a cold north-easterly wind, blowing along the east coast of Lancashire. The legend goes that Robin Hood couldn't bear any cold except that which a thawing wind brought with it.

Siling down Pouring down, raining heavily. The term is used most commonly in East Yorkshire and comes from the old Norse word *sila*, meaning to pour liquid through a strainer.

Smirr Scottish, meaning fine rain and drizzle.

Soft day Irish term for a grey, dull, misty day with rain expected.

Withershins (or widdershins) An old English term meaning to go anti-clockwise, literally 'against the sun'.

ONE OF A KIND

While our storms are now humanised with a name, there is only one named wind in the UK. The Helm Wind is a strong north-easterly which blows down the south-west slope of the Cross Fell range in the Cumbrian Pennines.

It is so-called because its arrival is heralded by a bank of cloud known as the Helm Cloud – from the word 'helmet' – which forms across the top of the fells. The wind can also be accompanied by a spectacular rolling cloud called the Helm Bar, which stays stationary but rotates as the downward gusts from the Helm Wind meet the warmer air below. In one part of the range, on the edge of the Eden Valley, a 600-metre drop causes the wind to intensify and the resulting roar is as loud as a high-speed train.

One of the earliest written references to the name was in the *Ipswich Reporter* on 15 November 1794, in a report about an asthmatic vicar who vacated his property because his doctor believed the fierce wind was exacerbating his condition. The report read:

His house stood on one of the highest mountains in England, where the wind, called the helm-wind, was excessively sharp and piercing. When he was at the communion table, his lungs were so much affected by the helm-wind that he fell down. He was unable to reside in that place, and therefore he removed from thence by the advice of his physician.

IDIOMS

Chatting about what a lovely day it is or moaning about the rain aren't the only times we might find ourselves talking about the weather. Many everyday phrases have their origin in meteorology and here's how some of them came about.

Brainstorm

E.g. 'Let's brainstorm ideas' or 'He had a brainstorm and came up with this solution.'

While we use the term to mean a clever idea that pops into the head, or the search for solutions and ideas, it originally meant something very different. In the nineteenth century, a brainstorm referred to a mental fit, such as an epileptic fit, or a moment of temporary insanity. The term comes from the idea of a storm or disturbance in the mind, similar to a thunderstorm, which prevents the afflicted from thinking normally.

Rain on my Parade

E.g. 'If she shows up to the party, she is going to rain on his parade.'

The phrase comes from a song sung by Barbra Streisand in the 1964 movie *Funny Girl*, entitled 'Don't Rain On My Parade'. In the late 1960s, it began to be used in speech and in newspaper articles and has since entered everyday speech.

Stealing Someone's Thunder

This phrase has a surprisingly literal story behind it. According to two accounts of the time, by Alexander Pope and playwright Colley Cibber, an actor and manager called John Dennis invented a machine that made the sound of thunder and debuted it in his play *Appius and Virginia*, at the Drury Lane Theatre in London in 1709.

The play was a flop and closed after a short run, to be replaced by a production of *Macbeth*. On the opening night, Dennis was furious to hear his thunder machine being used and reportedly stood up shouting, 'Damn them! They will not let my play run, but they steal my thunder.'

Fair Weather Friend

A person who only wants to be around you when times are good but disappears when you hit a rough patch. Thought to have been in use since the mid eighteenth century.

Under the Weather

A phrase meaning poorly or sick, it is believed to spring from an era when boat travel was common. Passengers suffering from seasickness during a storm would go below deck where the motion was less intense, so they were literally 'under the weather' other passengers were experiencing above deck.

As Right as Rain

Depending on your point of view, you might think there's nothing right about rain but the term is thought to derive from farmers, who depend on water for their crops.

The first literary use of the term appears in *The Real Charlotte* by Somerville and Ross in 1894: 'If only this infernal Fitzpatrick girl would have stayed with her cads in Dublin everything would have been as right as rain.'

Not Having the Foggiest (Idea)

Dickens was the first author recorded using 'foggy' to describe a thought or idea. In the 1841 novel *Barnaby Rudge*, he writes about a 'dull and foggy sort of idea', and it's thought that this expression has evolved to the modern-day 'I haven't the foggiest', meaning 'I don't know'.

Put the Wind up

The phrase 'to put the wind up somebody', meaning to alarm or frighten them, hails from the First World War and the talk of the trenches. In 1918, Wilfred Owen recalled 'Shells so close that they thoroughly put the wind up a Life Guardsman in the trench with me.'

According to etymologist Eric Partridge, the phrase came from the parody of a marching song called 'The British Grenadiers'. The version sung by the soldiers contained the line 'Father was a soldier, at the Battle of Waterloo, the wind blew up his trousers, and he didn't know what to do.' From that, anyone who was anxious or alarmed was said to 'have the wind up his trousers', which was later shortened to 'have (or get) the wind up'.

Get Wind of

To find out or discover something, e.g. 'If Mum gets wind of this, she won't be happy.' The phrase is thought to come from the way animals smell the wind for evidence of other animals nearby, sniffing out a predator or prey.

A Windfall

Originating in the fifteenth century, the term has now come to mean an unexpected fortune, such as an inheritance, a prize or large bonus. It originally referred to fruit or wood that was blown down by the wind and was therefore free to all.

Long-Winded

This comes from the 1580s and originally applied to someone who was 'given to lengthy speeches', the 'wind' referring to breath in speaking.

Storm in a Teacup

In the first century BC, Cicero referred to a 'tempest in a ladle' which is thought to be the precursor of this British phrase, meaning a disproportionate fuss about something trivial. In the USA, the term 'Tempest in a teacup' is more common. In the late eighteenth century, the British Lord Chancellor, Baron Thurlow, referred to an uprising in the Isle of Man as a 'tempest in a teapot' and around the same time Prime Minister Lord North used it to describe the protests of American colonists against the tea tax.

The first recorded instance of 'storm in teacup' occurs in Catherine Sinclair's *Modern Accomplishments* in 1838.

Spring Clean

The idea of giving the home a deep clean in the spring has different traditions in cultures around the world. Many historians trace the practice back to the ancient Jewish tradition of cleansing the house before the Feast of the Passover and others suggest links to the Iranian *Norouz*, the Persian new year, which falls on the first day of spring and is the traditional time for cleaning or 'shaking the house'. The Chinese also sweep the house to banish the past year's bad luck just before the Chinese new year.

In Europe and the USA, there are more pragmatic reasons for the spring clean. When houses were heated with coal and wood fires, soot, dust and grime would build up over the winter months. As soon as the spring weather arrived and it was warm enough to throw open the windows, the dirt could effectively be removed from furniture, carpets and walls, curtains washed and hung out to dry and bedding aired.

Like Greased Lightning

The phrase, used to describe something fast, has origins stretching back a lot further than the famous John Travolta song from the movie *Grease*. Based on the fact that if you add grease to anything it works faster, and the lightning bolt being the speediest of weather phenomena, it was used back in the 1800s and the earliest recorded use was in an English newspaper, the *Boston, Lincoln, Louth*

& Spalding Herald, in January 1833: 'He spoke as quick as greased lightning.'

Taking a Rain Check

A polite way of turning down an invitation or ducking out of a social arrangement, 'I'll take a rain check' actually comes from the world of American baseball. In the 1880s, if a match had to be called off because of a downpour, ticket holders were given a ticket for another game, known as a 'rain check'. In 1889, player Abner Powell came up with the idea of a detachable stub on tickets to prevent spectators who had sneaked in without a ticket from leaving with a rain check and this became a standard practice for all major league teams.

Sailing Close to the Wind

Another maritime expression, this refers to the fact that sailing boats can't sail directly into the wind but, to get more speed, they may sail as close to the direction of the wind as possible.

If they get the angle wrong, however, the wind may hit the back of the sail, causing the sail to 'luff' or flap in the breeze and the boat to lose speed and direction. The phrase has been adopted by landlubbers to mean taking a risk or coming close to danger.

Cloud Nine

Meaning exceptionally happy, as in 'She was on cloud nine after getting the new job'.

The origin of this is unclear but some theorists believe it refers to the 1896 *International Cloud Atlas*, which defined ten types of cloud. The ninth cloud, the cumulonimbus, was the highest in the sky, at 10 km (6.2 miles). Another theory is that it comes from traditional Chinese Han mythology, which divides the sky into nine layers. In Taoism, the ninth cloud is the highest layer, where the gods live.

WHY IS IT ALWAYS RAINING CATS AND DOGS?

Raining cats and dogs is a familiar phrase, trotted out whenever the rain is particularly torrential. Obviously this is not to be taken literally, as there has not yet been a recorded case of little fidos and tiddles falling from the sky on a rainy day. But the origin of the phrase has been the subject of much debate.

One popular but completely ridiculous theory circulated is that, in the sixteenth century, dogs and cats huddled in the thatched roofs of homes to keep warm and a heavy downpour would make them slide off. This is, of course, nonsense. Even if a cat liked to lie on the thatch, it is unlikely to stay there unless it's warm and dry and the idea of a dog living on the roof is absurd.

Another, more plausible theory is that the phrase derives from Norse mythology. Dogs and wolves were associated with Odin, the god of storms, and so were linked with rain, while cats were the familiars of witches, who flew broomsticks in the wind.

The most likely origin, though, comes from the seventeenth and eighteenth centuries, when heavy storms would wash all manner of disgusting debris through the filthy streets of British towns, including the carcasses of dead animals.

This theory would seem to be borne out in Jonathan Swift's poem 'A Description of a City Shower', published in *Tatler* magazine in 1710. Although the poem is a metaphor, denouncing London society, his description of flooded streets is no doubt an accurate one:

'Now in contiguous drops the flood comes down,
Threat'ning with deluge this devoted town ...

> *Sweeping from butchers' stalls, dung, guts, and blood,*
>
> *Drown'd puppies, stinking sprats, all drench'd in mud,*
>
> *Dead cats and turnip-tops come tumbling down the flood.'*

GLOBAL GOBBLEDYGOOK

The Brits aren't the only ones with odd and sometimes inexplicable phrases for a heavy downpour. There are many equivalent phrases, from 'raining troll women' to a slightly earthier French term which involves farmyard animals relieving themselves!

Here are some of the sayings used to describe rain around world.

Argentina: 'It's raining dung head-first.'

Australia: 'It's a frog strangling gully washer.'

China: 'Dog poo is falling.'

Denmark: 'It's raining cobbler boys,' or 'raining shoemakers' apprentices.'

Estonia: 'It's raining husbands.'

Faroe Islands: 'It's raining pilot whales.'

Finland: 'It's raining like Esther (or Esteri) sucks.'[1]

France: 'It's raining like a peeing cow.' (This is a polite translation for the real phrase *Il pleut comme vache qui pisse.*)

Germany: 'It's raining puppies.'

Greece: 'It's raining chair legs.'

Haiti: 'Dogs are drinking in their noses.'

Iceland: 'It's raining fire and brimstone.'

Ireland: 'It's throwing cobblers' knives.'

The Netherlands: 'It's raining old women,' and 'It's raining pipe-stems.'

Norway: 'It's raining troll women.'

Poland: 'It's raining frogs.'

Portugal and Brazil: 'It's raining frogs' beards.'

Serbia: 'The rain kills the mice.'

South Africa and Namibia: 'It's raining old women with knobkerries', meaning 'It's raining old women with clubs.'[2]

Thailand: 'It's raining ears and eyes shut.'

Wales: 'It's raining knives and forks.'

1. The origin of this is disputed. Some believe Esteri was the goddess of rain in pre-Christian Finland, but scholars have claimed this is untrue as the name is biblical. It is more likely to be a reference to an old brand of water pump used by the fire service.
2. In legend, old women cause various weather patterns by doing chores in heaven, such as shaking bed linen to make it snow and baking pancakes, to make it rain. The Knobkerrie is a thin weapon with a knob on the end which is also used as a walking stick.

THE NAMING OF THE SEASONS

Winter

The word 'winter' derives from the German word *wintar*, which is rooted in *wed*, meaning 'wet' or 'water', and referring to a wet season. The Anglo-Saxons counted age by winters, so a child could have been said to be 'three winters old'.

Spring

In the fourteenth century, nature's most fertile season was known as 'springing time', which referred to new plants 'springing' from the ground. Over time, that became 'spring time', and by the sixteenth century it was just 'spring'.

Summer

'Summer' came from the Old English name for that time of year, *sumor*, which was used before the year 900. This comes from the Germanic word *sumur*, and is similar to the Sanskrit word *samā*, meaning 'half-year'.

Autumn

Also known as 'harvest' in medieval times, the name comes from the Latin word *autumnus*, which relates to *augere*, meaning to increase and to have ample. This refers to the abundance of fruit, vegetables and grains which are harvested at this time of year.

The North American term 'fall' also originated in Britain, in the sixteenth century, and was the popular term for autumn throughout the seventeenth century. It literally referred to the falling of the leaves from the trees.

CHAPTER 4

A Lore Unto Itself

There are few subjects that feature in old wives' tales as much as the weather. The folklore surrounding the elements has built up over thousands of years as man attempts to predict the weather using signs from the natural world. Before the advent of technology, farmers planned their crops and harvests around the age-old sayings and many still swear by them today.

We all know the theory that cows lie down before rain and 'a red sky at night, shepherd's delight', but how many of these familiar phrases are actually true?

If it rains on St Swithun's Day, it will rain for forty days

St Swithun's Day falls on 15 July. A traditional rhyme states:

St Swithun's Day, if thou dost rain,

For forty days it will remain

St Swithun's Day, if thou be fair

For forty days 'twill rain nae mair.

St Swithun, the Bishop of Winchester, died in *c.*AD 862 and asked that he be buried in an ordinary grave outside the cathedral so that 'sweet rain from Heaven' would fall on it. Over a century later, on 15 July 971, monks who believed he had healing powers decided to move his remains to a shrine inside. On that day, Winchester was lashed with torrential rain which continued through forty days and was believed to have been caused by the disgruntled saint.

TRUE OR FALSE?

According to the Met Office there's not a lot of truth in this proverb. In fact there hasn't been a consecutive forty days of rain or of dry weather after 15 July since records began. It's not total bunkum, though: the Royal Meteorological Society says that weather patterns are often set in mid-July because that's when the jet stream settles down.

According to their research: 'If the jet stream lies north of the UK throughout the summer, continental high pressure is able to move in, bringing warmth and sunshine. If it sticks further south, Arctic air and Atlantic weather systems are likely to predominate, bringing colder, wetter weather.'

Ne'er cast your clout before may is out

This familiar saying, advises us never to take off our winter clothes until 'may is out', but it doesn't refer to the month of May, as many imagine. It actually refers to the blossom of the hawthorn bush, which usually flowers at the beginning of May.

TRUE OR FALSE?

The hawthorn is actually an excellent indicator of the coming of spring – if it flowers in April, you know the warm weather is coming earlier. So this old wives' tale is one you can take notice of.

Red sky at night, shepherd's delight
Red sky in the morning, shepherd's warning

This goes right back to biblical times, with a version appearing in the Gospel of Matthew:

He answered them, 'When it is evening, you say, "It will be fair weather, for the sky is red."'

The full saying relates to the colour of the sky at sunset and sunrise and how that indicates the weather over the next 24 hours.

TRUE OR FALSE?

In the UK, where most weather systems travel from west to east, this is a very reliable gauge of the coming weather, as a red sky at night means the setting sun will illuminate the departing clouds as a weather system moves away to the east and fair weather will follow.

A red sky is caused when the sun is low in the sky and sunlight is scattered by particles in the atmosphere illuminating the clouds in the sky with a bright orange and red glow. As the sun rises in the east and sets in the west, if a weather system is heading towards us in the morning, the low sun will illuminate the approaching clouds in the west, creating a red sky. If the sun is setting as a weather system exits then the resulting nocturnal red sky suggests that the system has passed and fair weather will follow.

This saying doesn't always work as not all weather systems travel west to east.

Rain before seven, fine by eleven

Thanks to a brisk westerly wind from the Atlantic, weather systems tend to move through the UK fairly rapidly, and this old wives' tale relies on this fact.

TRUE OR FALSE?

This one is a bit hit and miss. It may be true that early morning rain will clear by 11 a.m. but, as most people in the UK can testify, it can often stay around a lot longer, so it's not very reliable.

If St Michael brings many acorns, Christmas will cover the fields with snow

Michaelmas Day, or the feast of St Michael, falls on 29 September, at the end of the harvest season. Legend has it that the abundance of acorns can predict whether it will be a white Christmas.

TRUE OR FALSE?

There a solid foundation for this folklore as amateur climatologist David King explains. 'A lot of acorns means a harsh winter ahead,' he says. 'Acorns are an important source of food for birds when the ground is too hard for them to get worms, so nature makes sure they have enough food higher up.'

It is not, however, an accurate predictor of snow on 25 December, just of a very cold December.

If the cows are lying down, rain is on its way

A field full of cows, lying down, has long been thought to indicate rain later in the day, and there are a couple of theories as to why. One, the most likely, is that they like to keep a patch of grass dry during a downpour; another less-expounded theory is that they lie down to ease their stomachs, which are sensitive to a change in atmospheric pressure.

TRUE OR FALSE?

Sadly, neither theory is likely to be true. Cows lie down for a lot of reasons but not necessarily because of rain. According to *Farmers' Almanac*: 'Cows lying down in a field more often means they're chewing their cud, rather than preparing for raindrops.'

If a cat washes its face over its ear,
'Tis a sign the weather will be fine and clear

This saying may have originated from cats' behaviour in fine, dry weather which increases static electricity in their fur. This means they will moisten their fur more often to avoid irritation.

TRUE OR FALSE?

As pet lovers know, cats are meticulously clean animals and are constantly washing themselves, so their grooming is more likely to be a reaction to current conditions than a prediction of things to come. Interestingly enough, there is another old wives' tale which interprets the same grooming as a harbinger of rain: 'When a cat washes behind her ears, we'll soon be tasting Heaven's tears.'

WHUPPITY SCOORIE

The end of the harsh winter months is celebrated in Lanark, Scotland, with a traditional custom known as the Whuppity Scoorie. On 1 March, children with screwed-up balls of paper on a string gather at St Nicholas kirk where, at 6 p.m., a bell is rung. They then run three times round the church, clockwise, whooping loudly and swinging the balls above their heads.

Although it's uncertain when the tradition started, it was first mentioned in print in the *Hamilton Advertiser* in 1893 when it was reported to be at least 120 years old. Town officials believe the custom was intended to ward off evil spirits before the spring started.

If the goose honks low, rain is due
If the goose honks high, fair weather is due

There are many variations of this proverb which refers to the altitude that geese fly rather than the tone or pitch of their calls.

TRUE OR FALSE?

Geese fly at optimum air density, and the optimum density is higher during a period of high pressure. In times of low pressure, which brings bad weather, the opposite is true – so low-flying geese are generally bad news.

If the Ash before the Oak, there'll be a summer soak,
But if the Oak before the Ash, there'll only be
a splash

This saying refers to the time of year that the ash tree and oak tree grow their leaves. The oak can leaf any time between late March and May, and the ash tends to leaf around April–May. The proverb suggests that if the oak leaves sprout first, we can look forward to a wet summer.

TRUE OR FALSE?

Oak trees are very sensitive to temperature and an early warm spring will bring on the leafing earlier in the year.

If oak is late it indicates a cold spring. Ash is less affected by temperature so will leaf after the oak during a warm spring.

When it comes to the amount of rain the following summer will bring, however, research by the Met Office and the Woodland Trust has concluded there is no truth in the proverb.

If spiders are spinning webs, fair weather is on the way

This prediction applies more to spiders building webs outside than inside, which many see as an omen of good weather ahead.

TRUE OR FALSE?

There is certainly an element of truth in this, in that spiders' webs absorb water and rain and humid weather will cause them to become saturated and break. When spiders sense high humidity, they are likely to stay hidden. If, however, they sense dry air it's prime hunting time, so they will spin webs to catch those unsuspecting insects enjoying the sunshine.

How far in advance their predictive skills stretch is unclear, but they will abandon webs at the first drop of rain.

Halo around the sun or moon, rain or snow is coming soon

A bright ring seen around these heavenly bodies has long been seen as a portent to less than heavenly weather.

TRUE OR FALSE?

The halo effect is caused by refraction of the light through the ice crystals of high cirrus clouds, which often indicates a warm front is approaching, along with an associated area of low pressure. This doesn't necessarily mean rain or snow every time, but it is highly likely.

Ice in November to bear a duck, for the rest of the year there'll be slush and muck

This saying suggests that when ponds are cold enough in November to freeze over, the rest of the winter will be wet and mild, bringing slush and muck rather than ice and snow.

TRUE OR FALSE?

Sadly, it doesn't appear that this icy theory holds water. Looking at records over the last fifty years or so shows that exceptionally cold Novembers are followed by cold winters as often as they are by mild ones, and by average temperatures even more often. Between 1925 and 2010, sixteen very mild winters were preceded by one mild, twelve average, and three cold Novembers.

The Met Office stats since then also prove the duck is no predictor of things to come. A spokesman revealed: 'In 2010 we had an exceptionally cold winter, at 1.9°C below average, but the rest of the winter months, January, February and March, were also extremely cold, at 2.09°C below average. The winters in between have either been mild both in November and for the whole winter, or around average. Only the winter of 2016 – when November was 1.3°C below average and the winter was 1.8°C above – fits the bill for the duck theory.'

STONEHENGE

The original purpose of the ancient standing stones at Stonehenge is still under debate, but many believe it is all about the sun. The Salisbury Plain monument was built between 3000 and 1600 BC, and various studies have concluded that the entire alignment of the site points to the sunrise of the summer solstice and the sunset of the winter solstice,

During summer solstice in June, thousands still flock there to watch the sunrise. If you stand inside the circle, looking north-east through the entrance, the sun rises directly above a rough stone outside the circle – known as the Heel Stone. Some believe the name 'heel' originated from the Greek *helios*, meaning sun.

Winter solstice, or the shortest day, falls around 20 December, when there is another spectacular sight to be seen at Stonehenge. On this day, the sun sets in the centre of three great stones – known as the Trilithon – consisting of two large vertical stones supporting a third, horizontal stone across the top.

The alignment seems to indicate that the ancient civilisations who laid the stones were in thrall to the sun, and hardly surprising. The seasons – governed by the sun's position – affected every aspect of their lives, from the growing and harvesting of crops to the life cycle of their livestock.

Modern-day architects have learned a thing or two from the ancient builders' designs. Milton Keynes's central road is designed so that when the sun rises on the solstice it shines straight down Midsummer Boulevard and reflects in the glass of the train station.

CHAPTER 5

Since Records Began

Whenever the mercury hits the high numbers or the rain gets particularly torrential, weather experts reach for past figures to see if a new benchmark has been set. It's then that the familiar phrase 'Since records began' is heard. But when *did* they begin?

The answer is not as cut and dried as you might think. In fact, even within the Met Office, there are many different dates, depending on the type of weather and accuracy of data required – with some information going back as far as 1659. For the more accurate readings, however, the Met Office uses a digital system with more recent data.

THE UK CLIMATE SERIES

While the archive material stretches back centuries, the digitised system, which relies on a huge amount of data from every weather station across the UK, dates back to 1910 for temperature and rainfall, and later for other measurements. Data is recorded at 5 km grid points, taking into account geographical features such as hills and valleys and environment, i.e. urban or rural. These are then used to produce a series of figures such as average maximum temperature, rainfall amount and hours of sunshine.

So the records for each are as follows:

1910 – UK and regional temperature and precipitation
1929 – UK and regional sunshine duration
1961 – UK and regional variables, such as frost, cloud
    cover, wind and snow

THE HADLEY CENTRE SERIES

A system to study climate change, developed at the Met Office Hadley Centre, takes data from selected stations representing large regions. They are divided into the Central England Temperature series (HadCET) and the United Kingdom Precipitation series (HadUKP).

Records go back as far as 1659, and much of the information that pre-dates the twentieth century is gleaned from the weather diaries of amateur meteorologists. The National Meteorological Archive in Exeter holds the personal observation logs from thousands of people which don't just record the weather, but effects on wildlife and plants in regions of the country.

Since Hadley was opened in 1990, meteorologists have been working through these vast archives to check their validity and input the data on to a computer.

THE CENTRAL ENGLAND TEMPERATURE SERIES (HADCET)

Using a small number of stations from the Midlands to Lancashire, the series collects data for maximum, minimum and mean temperature, daily and monthly. Start dates:

1659 – Mean temperature, monthly

1772 – Mean temperature, daily

1878 – Maximum and minimum temperature, daily and monthly

THE UK PRECIPITATION SERIES (HADUKP)

Using around eighty selected stations, about 3 per cent of the working stations, this programme analyses data for nine UK regions – three in Scotland, five in England and Wales and one in Northern Ireland. Start dates:

1766 – England and Wales, monthly

1873 – Five sub-regions of England and Wales, monthly

1931 – Scotland, three Scottish sub-regions and Northern Ireland, monthly

1931 – England and Wales, Scotland, Northern Ireland and eight sub-regions

SIZZLING SUMMERS

The hottest temperature recorded in the UK was in Faversham, Kent, on 10 August 2003 when the mercury hit 38.5°C. But that balmy day wasn't part of the hottest summer ever. For that, we have to go back some forty years, to the long hot summer of 1976, when Britons basked in beautiful sunshine for two months.

The heatwave set in around 20 June, and in the following weeks temperatures continued to rise across most of mainland Britain. In fact, between 23 June and 7 July the temperature topped 32°C in at least one UK weather centre for fifteen consecutive days.

The average temperature between June and August was 17.8°C and the average maximum temperature was 20.96°C. This scorching summer included the hottest June day ever, with a high of 35.6°C recorded in Southampton on 28 June, and the highest temperature recorded all summer was at Cheltenham on 3 July, at 35.9°C.

It all sounds idyllic but the heatwave came at a price. The UK was hit by a drought, with Devon and Dorset having no rainfall for forty-five days. Water rationing was brought in, and many were forced to use standpipes in the street. In parts of Wales, supplies were cut off for seventeen hours a day for eleven weeks, and the lack of rain caused £500 million worth of damage to crops resulting in soaring food prices. It even led to considerable damage to property, through subsidence caused by parched ground – and insurance companies footed a bill for £60 million.

It was the driest summer since 1776, with rainfall of just 74 mm. But that record was surpassed in 1995 when just 73 mm fell.

STANDPIPES AND STAND-OFFS

The summer of 1995 saw a prolonged period of twenty-seven days without rainfall between 27 July and 22 August and only 1 mm of rain in the whole of August. The resulting drought meant nothing more than hosepipe bans in parts of the UK but for one region, West Yorkshire, the dry spell sparked its very own storm.

The Pennine reservoirs owned by Yorkshire Water ran dry and 1,000 tankers had to be brought in to ferry water from the east of the county, 24 hours a day. Standpipes were erected in the street and a National Rivers Association report revealed that the company planned to apply for an emergency drought order to implement a rota, which would see residents having their supplies disconnected for 24 hours, every second day, on a rota system.

Amid reports that the company was losing a third of its treated water from leaky pipes, there was outrage amongst customers and reports of officials being threatened as they erected standpipes. This wasn't helped by Yorkshire Water's chief executive demonstrating how to wash thoroughly in a basin of water and claiming he hadn't bathed for three months – before being caught going to friends and relatives outside the county to bath, according to the *Yorkshire Post*.

The company was summoned to Parliament to explain itself, and both the CEO and the Chairman stood down. The drought led to the company investing £250 million in a network of pipelines to bring in water from other parts of the country, should another drought occur.

We're a small country with big variations in the weather. We sit with the Atlantic to our west, the vast expanse of the continent to our east, and both have a part to play in our weather. Things can change very quickly, from hour to hour and minute to minute, and so our weather is very interesting to people.

Ben Rich, weather presenter

THE LONG DROUGHT

The dry summer of 1995 kicked off a three-year hydrological drought, when warm dry summers were followed by dry winters, meaning the reservoirs emptied and the water table fell. Even one of the soggiest summers in history – 1998, with 34 per cent above average rainfall – failed to end the drought because, as *The Independent*

reported, it was the 'wrong kind of rain'. In other words, it was being soaked up by the topsoil and evaporating again without percolating through to the water table and topping up the rivers and reservoirs.

The water levels only rose again in an exceptionally wet period between 1999 and 2002, but a similar cycle began in 2003, with three years of dry summers and winters leading to low water levels and controversial hosepipe bans in the south of England. Among the banned activities were car washing, watering the garden, filling private swimming pools and hot-tubs and hosing down driveways and patios. There was widespread anger at the bans, which many saw as a result of inefficiency and an inability to move water from one part of the country to another.

Another drought hit southern England in 2012 after a two-year dry spell. The worst hit were the Thames Valley and London areas, which received below average rainfall for eighteen of the twenty-four months from 2010 to 2011, and East Anglia, which suffered the driest six months since 1921. Seven water companies introduced bans but again there was widespread anger when OFWAT revealed that many of them had failed to hit their leakage targets and that water companies across England and Wales had leaked 3,365 million litres a day in 2010 and 2011.

CAR TROUBLE

During a blazing hot July in 1921, an eagle-eyed Metropolitan Water Board inspector noticed an excessive amount of water pouring down a gutter in an exclusive Belgravia mews. He investigated further and discovered chauffeur Joseph Gorton washing his employer's car with a hosepipe which was 'thrown down by the side of it, the water still running'. As the country was suffering a drought, this wasteful behaviour landed the poor man in court and a fine of 20 shillings – the equivalent of £260 today. This was the first recorded prosecution under a hosepipe ban.

THE UK'S HIGHEST RECORDED TEMPERATURES

England	38.5°C	101.3°F	Faversham, Kent	10 August 2003
Wales	35.2°C	95.3°F	Hawarden Bridge, Flintshire	2 August 1990
Scotland	32.9°C	91.2°F	Greycrook, Scottish Borders	9 August 2003
Northern Ireland	30.8°C	87.4°F	Knockarevan, County Fermanagh	30 June 1976
			Shaw's Bridge, Belfast, County Antrim	12 July 1983

(Source: The Met Office)

GLOBAL WARMING

The hottest year on record, globally, was 2016. According to NASA, the World Meteorological Organization and scientists at the Met Office Hadley Centre, temperatures were up 1.1°C above those of the pre-industrial period (1850–1900). The new highs narrowly beat the record temperatures set in 2015, just one year before – which had been the hottest since 1850.

Although some of the added heat (0.2°C) was attributed to El Niño, Peter Stott, Acting Director of the Met Office Hadley Centre, concluded: 'The main contributor to warming over the last 150 years is human influence on climate from increasing greenhouse gases in the atmosphere.'

GREEN AND SOGGY LAND

High in the Cumbrian hills, in the stunning scenery of the Lake District, lies the Honister Pass. As well as being one of the highest and steepest passes in the region, it boasts the dubious honour of being the wettest place in Britain. On 5 December 2015, this ramblers' paradise took a battering with 341.4 mm of rain in 24 hours – from 6 a.m. to 6 a.m. – breaking records for one day of rainfall.

The record for the wettest standard 'rainfall day' – measured from 9 a.m. to 9 a.m. – goes to the pretty village of Martinstown in Dorset, which received a deluge measuring 279 mm on 18 July 1955.

RECORD-BREAKING RAIN

Duration	Level	Location	Date
Highest 5-min total	Approx. 32 mm	Preston, Lancashire	10 August 1893
Highest 30-min total	80 mm	Eskdalemuir, Dumfries and Galloway	26 June 1953
Highest 60-min total	92 mm	Maidenhead, Berkshire	12 July 1901
Highest 90-min total	117 mm	Dunsop Valley, Lancashire	8 August 1967
Highest 120-min total	155 mm	Hewenden Reservoir, West Yorkshire	11 June 1956
Highest 155-min total	169 mm	Hampstead, London	14 August 1975
Highest 180-min total	178 mm	Horncastle, Lincolnshire	7 October 1960
Highest 24-hour total	341.4 mm	Honister Pass, Cumbria	5 December 2015
Highest 48-hour total	405 mm	Thirlmere, Cumbria	4–5 December 2015
Highest 72-hour total	456.4 mm	Seathwaite, Cumbria	17–19 November 2009

| Highest 96-hour total | 495 mm | Seathwaite, Cumbria | 16–19 November 2009 |
| Highest Monthly Total | 1396.4 mm | Crib Goch, Snowdon | 1–31 December 2015 |

(Source: The Met Office)

THEN CAME THE FLOODS

The winter of 2015–2016 was a complete washout, with November to January recorded as the wettest three months in the UK since 1910. When Storm Desmond hit, on 5 December 2015, the result was devastating floods in many parts of the UK. In Lancashire and Cumbria, where a month's rain fell in a day, over 6,000 homes were flooded as waters reached a record 8-metre height. Many residents had to be rescued by boat – including some who were picked up from the roofs of their houses. Thousands more homes lost power because of a waterlogged sub-station in Lancaster. In Calderdale, West Yorkshire, 2,000 homes were flooded and over 1,000 in Leeds were inundated when the River Aire burst its banks.

More misery was in store over Christmas when Storm Eva, Desmond's little sister, hit parts of the UK. Cumbria was once more deluged by floods, with villages such as Appleby and Keswick finding themselves under 90 cm (3 feet) of water and Glenridding flooded for the third time in a month. In North Yorkshire, the bridge across the River Wharfe collapsed, splitting town in two and leaving a £4.4 million reconstruction bill. In Shannon in Ireland, 6,000 homes were left without power. The storms and floods left a total insurance bill of more than £1.3bn.

The Centre for Ecology and Hydrology (CEH), in collaboration with the British Hydrological Society, studied the storms and found that rivers across northern England, Scotland and Northern Ireland had record peak flows in those three winter months. Their report said that the Eden, Tyne and Lune had record peaks of about 1,700 cubic metres per second – enough to fill London's Royal Albert Hall in less than a minute.

Author Terry Marsh said: 'The associated flooding was both extensive and repetitive, and total river outflows from Great Britain following the passage of Storm Desmond in December exceeded the previous maximum by a substantial margin.'

AN ILL WIND

The strongest wind ever recorded in the UK was a fierce 173 mph (150 knots). Not many felt it, as it was gauged at the summit of Cairngorm mountain, in the Scottish Highlands on 20 March 1986. In fact, anyone brave enough to have climbed it that day would have had a hard time staying on the mountain at all. Gusts of 142 mph (123.4 knots) were recorded at Fraserburgh in Aberdeenshire on 13 February 1989, and of 124 mph (107.8 knots) on 12 January 1974 at Kilkeel in County Down.

The five windiest areas of the UK, based on the 1981–2010 annual average wind speed, are:

1. Shetland Area   17 mph (14.7 knots)
2. Buteshire   16.7 mph (14.5 knots)
3. Orkney Area   16.5 mph (14.3 knots)
4. Caernarvonshire   14.8 mph (12.9 knots)
5. Western Isles   14.5 mph (12.6 knots)

MULLING IT OVER

In 2016, locals on the Isle of Mull, in the Inner Hebrides, noticed a spectacular effect caused by Storm Henry: gales of 90 mph blowing up in a rocky area known as the Wilderness managed to turn a waterfall upside down so that it flowed up and over a cliff edge. Footage recorded

by Reuben O'Connell, director of the Isle of Mull cottages, went viral and was viewed by millions online.

While incredible to watch, the phenomenon is not unique and has also been observed at other steep waterfalls, such as the Kinder Falls in Derbyshire's Peak District and County Moher in Ireland.

I think we're so obsessed by the weather in the UK because we live in a location where we can literally experience all four seasons of weather in one day!

The UK is such an interesting place to forecast for as we are surrounded by water in the mid latitudes where

a simple change in the wind direction can bring us differing weather. One day we might be forecasting a north westerly wind which will bring cool, moist arctic air bringing us a chilly and wet day but the next, the wind can be from the south east bringing warm and dry conditions.

Most of us like to spend time outside, whether it be playing sport, having a BBQ, a walk or heading to the shops ... Knowing when we need to cancel our plans or take an umbrella because of rain is vitally important.

Simon King, weather presenter

WINTER

The coldest temperature recorded in the UK since 1961 is Braemar in Scotland, where the mercury plummeted to –27.2 °C, on 10 January 1982. Since then, Altnaharra, in Northern Scotland, is the only other weather station to record this low, on 30 December 1995. Not surprisingly, Scotland tops the league for its freezing conditions with nine out of the lowest eleven scores being recorded north of the border.

	Date	Station	Area	Temperature
1	10 January 1982	Braemar	East Scotland	−27.2°C
1	30 December 1995	Altnaharra No 2	North Scotland	−27.2°C
3	13 December 1981	Shawbury	Midlands	−25.2°C
4	13 January 1979	Carnwath	West Scotland	−24.6°C
5	20 January 1984	Grantown-On-Spey	East Scotland	−23.6°C
6	27 January 1985	Lagganlia	North Scotland	−23.4°C
7	13 January 1987	Caldecott P Sta	Midlands	−23.3°C
8	08 January 2010	Altnaharra No 2	North Scotland	−22.3°C
9	18 February 1960	Grantown-On-Spey	East Scotland	−22.2°C
9	30 December 1961	Cannich	North Scotland	−22.2°C
9	18 January 1963	Braemar	East Scotland	−22.2°C

(Source: The Met Office)

LET IT SNOW

Snow or sleet falls in the UK, on average, for 23.7 days a year, based on figures since 1981, but much of this falls on higher ground, where the temperature is lower. As well as being the coldest part of the UK, Scotland is also the snowiest, with 38.1 days of snow on average and the Cairngorms is the snowiest place of all, with a whopping 76.2 days of snow – three times the national average.

If the white stuff is not your thing, Cornwall is the place for you – as they are blessed with just 7.4 days' snowfall a year.

When it comes to ground cover, however, there are not many days when the sledges can be dragged out of the shed. Snow lies on the ground across the UK for just 15.6 days a year, rising to 26.2 days in Scotland, and most of that is in the mountains.

Snow in April or even May is not uncommon, but in 1975 several cricket matches had to be cancelled across the country because of snow showers – on 2 June!

In 1947, snow fell somewhere in the UK every day from 22 January to 17 March, making it the snowiest winter of the twentieth century.

DEADLY AVALANCHE

A severe winter in 1836–1837 brought blizzards and freezing temperatures to the whole of the UK, and the harsh weather resulted in a tragedy in one Sussex town. Over the Christmas period, snowdrifts accumulated on the South Downs. Driven by gale-force winds, snowdrifts 3 metres (10 feet) high were forming. One such drift built up on a cornice at Cliffe Hill, in Lewes, above a settlement of workers' cottages called Boulder Row.

On Boxing Day, a large amount of snow fell from the cornice into a nearby builder's yard, owned by a Mr Willes, destroying his sawing shed. Willes immediately warned the residents of Boulder Row to evacuate their homes, but they refused. The following morning they were once more advised to leave, as meteorologist Dr Charles Leeson-Prince recorded in an 1893 book:

> *The danger was then so evident that several persons went to the inmates and endeavoured to persuade them to leave the houses.*
>
> *Some of them came out, but others, although places of safety were offered to them, persisted in remaining and endeavouring to remove their effects.*
>
> *At about a quarter past ten a young man named Robert Hyam, who had by courageously scaling the declivity stood close under the impending mass of snow and ascertained the danger, rushed, together with Mr Morris, into the general passage of the buildings and implored the inmates not to lose a moment if they wished to save their lives.*
>
> *The poor creatures, however, appeared to be bewildered and would not depart. Hyam endeavoured to drag two*

women out by force, but was compelled to desist in order to save his own life.

He had scarcely got clear of the buildings when a huge field of solid snow toppled on the brink, and sliding down the steep hill with tremendous force, threw down and completely buried the seven end houses.

When the mist of snow cleared off not a vestige of a habitation was to be seen — nothing but an enormous mass of pure white.

Fifteen people were buried in the avalanche and, despite an immediate rescue attempt launched by the locals, eight lost their lives. A pub which now stands on the site of the cottages was named the Snowdrop Inn, in memory of the victims.

THE BIG FREEZE

The winter of 1962–1963 was not the coldest on record, but it was the coldest since 1740. With temperatures dropping below −20°C on frequent occasions, the arctic conditions meant that rivers and lakes froze over and, in Herne Bay in Kent, the sea froze over up to a mile out from the coast. In Dunkirk, across the North Sea, the ice reached out four miles and the BBC even voiced concern that the Strait of Dover would completely freeze over. Icicles of over a metre (3 feet) hung on houses, and in Oxford a car was driven over the frozen Thames.

The harsh winter also brought blizzards in December, with snowdrifts of up to 6 metres (20 feet) in parts of the country.

FROST FAIRS

During a 500-year cold snap known as the 'Little Ice Age', from the fourteenth to the nineteenth century, it was not uncommon for the Thames to completely freeze over. On seven such occasions, the ice was so thick it prompted an impromptu festival, known as the 'frost fair', where Londoners would gather on it, drinking, eating and even dancing on it.

The first recorded frost fair was during the winter of 1607–1608 when the river froze in December, allowing people to walk between Southwark and the City. By January the ice was so thick people congregated on it and set up camp, with makeshift shops, fruit sellers plying their trade and even tented pubs, selling liquor to the revellers.

The winter of 1683–1684 was even harsher, causing the river to freeze for two months and facilitating the most famous of the fairs, the Blanket Fair. On 6 January 1684, diarist John Evelyn noted that the ice had 'now become so thick as to beare not onely streetes of boothes in which they roasted meate, and had divers shops of wares quite acrosse as in a towne, but coaches, carts, and horses passed over. At this time there was a footpassage quite over the river, from Lambeth-stairs to the Horse-ferry at Westminster and hackney coaches began to carry fares from Somerset House and the Temple to Southwark.'

Evelyn also described the hedonistic pursuits of the locals as, 'bull-baiting, horse and coach races, puppet plays and interludes, cookes, tipling and other lewd places, so that it seemed a bacchanalian triumph or carnival on the water.' King Charles II was said to have attended the fair, and tucked into an ox that was spit-roasted on the ice.

The winter fairs took place until 1814, when a four-day party was held in February. Gin and ale was liberally drunk in temporary pubs known as 'fuddling tents' because of the effect of the alcohol in the drinkers, oxen were roasted and nine-pin bowling was played. In fact, the ice was so thick that an elephant was led across the river, just beside London Bridge, without a crack appearing.

Some of the festival-goers who ventured too far down the river did end up in the water but there were no reports of any fatalities at the final fair. This wasn't always the case, however. In 1715, an apple-seller known as Doll the Pippin woman fell through the ice and died, prompting a rhyme in Gay's *Trivia*:

> *'Pippins,' she cries, but Death her voice confounds*
> *And pip, pip, pip, along the ice resounds.*

During the 1739 fair, a large section of ice gave way and many were drowned in the Thames, and in 1789 melting ice caused a moored ship to break away, pulling down a Rotherhithe pub where it had literally laid its anchor. An article in *Gentleman's Magazine* explained:

> *The captain of a vessel lying off Rotherhithe, the better to*
> *secure the ship's cables, made an agreement with a publican for*
> *fastening a cable to his premises. In consequence, a small anchor*
> *was carried on shore, and deposited in the cellar, while another*

97

cable was fastened round a beam in another part of the house. In the night the ship veered about, and the cables holding fast, carried away the beam, and levelled the house with the ground, by which accident five persons asleep in their beds were killed.

CHAPTER 6

The Forecast Factory

Predicting the weather has changed dramatically since Aristotle's day and has come on leaps and bounds since Admiral FitzRoy's early gale warnings. Huge advances in technology mean meteorologists have progressed from observing and recording weather patterns to analysing them and predicting future events.

Today, the Met Office has a vast observation network and a range of high-tech equipment to help it in its quest for perfect predictions. So just how are the weather forecasts actually put together?

For each forecast there are four major steps – observation, assimilation, the numerical model and the final calculations, made by a supercomputer.

STEP 1: OBSERVATION

For the Met Office, the daily flow of observations is the most vital part of forecasting. It receives around 500,000 recordings of atmospheric conditions around the world every day, 24 hours a day, which are then passed on to the major forecasting centres in other countries. Readings are taken from the highest heights – 36,000 km above the Earth – to the depths of the oceans – 2,000 km under the sea. They are gathered in many different ways and cover temperature, pressure, wind speed and direction, humidity and many other details which provide the starting point for the forecast.

Land, Sea and Air

The Met Office has over 200 automatic land-based weather stations in the UK, which take readings on an hourly basis, and a similar number of manual stations. They provide an overview of the weather fronts moving through the country which forms the base of the synoptic chart. They are situated around 40 km apart and must be on level ground with no trees or steep slopes nearby that could influence the readings. They can't be placed near buildings to avoid the warming effect of artificial heating, near shade which would affect the measurement of sunshine or on top of a hill where wind would be stronger than the surrounding area.

For readings at sea, surface data is collected from ships and buoys in coastal areas around the UK.

Automatic reporting systems on board aircraft also measure temperature and wind and provide the results through the AMDAR (Aircraft Meteorological DAta Relay) programme.

Weather Balloons and Radiosondes

A radiosonde is a small battery-powered device that is sent up into the air by a helium-filled balloon, or weather balloon, on a daily basis. It typically ascends at a rate of 5 metres per second and, as it does, it sends data on temperature, humidity and wind to a receiver every two seconds. On average it will reach a height of 25 km before the drop in pressure causes the balloon to burst and the radiosonde to drop to the ground with the aid of a small parachute, with a GPS tracking its whereabouts.

The first radiosonde was launched in January 1929 in France by Robert Bureau, who also named the device. A year later a more practical version, developed independently by Russian Pavel Molchanov, was launched and quickly became the standard because it converted its readings into Morse code, making it more user-friendly.

In Finland, Professor Vilho Vaisala was busy designing his own version and, after first flying it in 1931, he established a company to make and market his device in 1936. Today, the Vaisala company is the largest producer of radiosondes in the world, and the Met Office currently uses the Vaisala RS92 radiosondes, as do many meteorological services around the world, including the US National Weather Service.

The Met Office now has six operational launching sites in the UK of which two – Lerwick in Shetland and Camborne in Cornwall – are manned. The other four, which are automatic, are in Castor Bay (Northern Ireland), Watnall (Nottingham), Herstmonceux (south of London) and Albemarle (near Newcastle).

Although radiosondes and weather balloons provide accurate readings, their landings are not always so accurate. They have been known to get caught in power lines, crack the occasional windscreen and even break panes of glass in conservatories. The Met Office do pay for any damages which occur and say the incidents are few and far between, with someone putting in a claim about every six months. Not bad considering they launch 3,500 balloons a year.

Satellites

Since the early models of the 1960s and 1970s, the weather satellite has become an invaluable tool in the forecasting armoury. They can be polar orbiting, meaning they circle the Earth on a north-south orbit, or geostationary, which means they hover over the same spot on the equator.

From their space vantage point, the satellites send back clear images of cloud cover and movement as well as capturing fires, effects of pollution, sand and dust storms, snow cover, ice mapping and boundaries of ocean currents. They also help to monitor the activity of live volcanoes and ash clouds.

The devices use two different areas of the electromagnetic spectrum – visible light and infrared or thermal images. Visible light images show clear pictures of lakes, forests and mountains as well as clouds, fog and smog, while the thermal imaging uses sensors called radiometers to measure cloud heights and types, temperatures on land and surface water and chart ocean features.

Countries and agencies from around the world collaborate to share the information provided by the weather satellites and maximise their future development. The Met Office represents the UK in the EUMETSAT (European Organisation for the Exploitation of Meteorological Satellites), a group made up of thirty countries that pool resources in order to launch and maintain meteorological satellites and distribute their findings. Weather data from these satellites, as well as those run by the USA, Japan and Russia, is shared among 191 member states of the World Meteorological Organization, or WMO, an agency of the United Nations.

LOVE IS IN THE AIR

The scientists at the Met Office have been known to reveal their sunny outlook from time to time. For example, on fourteen February 2017, meteorologist Alex Deakin celebrated Valentine's Day by slipping the titles of fourteen love songs into his 90-second forecast. The video – which had Alex mentioning classic ballads by Elvis Presley, Bette Midler, Lionel Richie and many more – went viral and received much praise on social media.

Here's Alex's now famous Valentine's Day forecast. How many love songs can you spot?

Hello. A change with the weather this week as we look towards the Atlantic to the milder air and we say hello, wave goodbye to the colder conditions – that bitter wind beneath my wings and everywhere else. So indeed by midweek we should be up where we belong temperature-wise.

If you've been wishing on a star for some of the wet stuff then yes, there will be some rain around. For most of us though it's dry for the rest of Tuesday and if you cherish the sunshine then you're in luck in the east. Further south and west there's most cloud around and that cloud providing rain as we zoom into Wales and parts of the Midlands.

Now, temperatures are always on my mind and it's going to be another cold one in the east, just six or seven degrees here, but further south we should reach double figures — 10 to maybe 13 in the far south west.

So for the romantics amongst you, will it be wonderful tonight as we run through this evening? Actually most places are going to be dry all night long with clouds spreading their way further north, clearer in the south, and of course the far north of Scotland. If you were here tonight we could just see some touches of frost but most places staying up at five or six degrees Celsius.

Time after time through this winter we've been talking about dry weather in the UK and it looks like we'll see more of the same as we move closer towards the weekend. It looks largely dry with lighter winds and instead of two sparrows in a hurricane the weather looks an awful lot calmer.

Answers on the next page

VALENTINE'S DAY ANSWERS

Here are the 14 love songs Alex Deakin slipped in. Did you spot them all?

1. 'Hello' – Lionel Richie
2. 'Say Hello, Wave Goodbye' – Soft Cell
3. 'Wind Beneath My Wings' – Bette Midler
4. 'Up Where We Belong' – Joe Cocker and Jennifer Warnes
5. 'Wishing On A Star' – Rose Royce
6. 'Cherish' – Madonna
7. 'Zoom' – Fat Larry's Band
8. 'Always On My Mind' – Elvis Presley
9. 'Wonderful Tonight' – Eric Clapton
10. 'All Night Long' – Lionel Richie
11. 'If You Were Here Tonight' – Alexander O'Neal
12. 'Time After Time' – Cyndi Lauper
13. 'Move Closer' – Phyllis Nelson
14. 'Two Sparrows In A Hurricane' – Tanya Tucker

STEP 2: ASSIMILATION

While today's sophisticated instruments provide readings from most areas, there are still some parts of the ocean and atmosphere which remain out of reach, and that's where assimilation comes in. Meteorologists factor in all the observations they do have to estimate what conditions will be like in the areas that they don't have data for.

STEP 3: NUMERICAL MODELS

Numerical weather prediction (NWP) is a computer model of the atmosphere that provides the basis of modern forecasts. Using the laws of physics and the data from the observation and assimilations, it uses a set of complex equations to predict the weather ahead. It does this by using a set of mathematical equations which can be read by a super computer, to advance 'chunks' over geographical areas (grid boxes) and through steps in time.

STEP 4: THE SUPERCOMPUTERS GO TO WORK

Even the sharpest brain in meteorology couldn't wade through the billions of figures thrown up by the numerical weather predictions. But state-of-the-art supercomputers, which can convert these equations in a matter of minutes, mean that weather forecasts are quicker and more accurate than ever before. In fact a four-day forecast now is as reliable as a one-day forecast was thirty years ago.

The Met Office currently uses a Cray Supercomputer which can process more than 16,000 trillion calculations a second. That means a five-day forecast can be produced in a few hours.

The Long and Short of It

For short-range forecasts, as with long-range, the NWP is used, but the difference is the size of the grid boxes. The current global forecast model solves 160 million equations just to predict fifteen minutes of atmospheric changes in a 40-km grid box. But for a short-range prediction, more localised details are required, meaning the size of the grid is reduced to 12.5 km.

Nowcasting

Although the term was first coined in 1980 by Met Office scientist Professor Keith Browning, nowcasting relies on the techniques Admiral FitzRoy first employed some 120 years earlier. It takes a snapshot of the current weather and, using estimates of wind speed and direction, predicts where the weather fronts will move to in the hours ahead.

The most useful application is to predict the movement of rain, hail and snow and, while winter rain bands can be predicted accurately for up to four hours, the less predictable summer storms are only forecasted two hours ahead.

Today, the Met Office uses a computer programme called the Short Term Ensemble Prediction System (STEPS), developed in collaboration with the Australian Bureau of Meteorology. This produces many forecasts using data about both large and small rainfall events, and shows the areas which move at different speeds. The advantage of the method is its speed and accuracy, allowing the Met Office to update its forecast every hour and constantly update any flood warnings in place.

PENNIES FROM HEAVEN

The work of the Met Office is publicly funded and a government report, commissioned in 2015, came to the conclusion that it more than paid its way. The weather warnings and forecasts, it was estimated, saved the nation between £1 billion and £1.5 billion in limiting flood and storm damage, helping airlines plan and helping to boost the economy.

This table of the various sectors showed just how much money was saved in each area.

Sector	Value (per annum)
Public	£480m
Aviation	£400m
Land Transport	£100m
Flood damage avoidance	£64m
Storm damage avoidance	£80m
Added value to the Economy	£400m

The sum of the benefits itemised is £1.52 bn per annum.

Saving Lives

On top of the monetary benefits, the report found that, while it was hard to put a figure on it, the work of the Met Office saved 'tens of lives' from the 'direct impacts of the weather' every year.

The total cost of the Public Weather Service (PWS) in that year came to £119.7m – less than 10 per cent of the calculated benefits.

The report concluded: 'We can state with very high confidence that the economic benefits of the PWS to the UK are in excess of £1bn per annum. The benefits attributable to the PWS are more likely to be around £1.5bn, and for weather services as a whole the benefits are likely to exceed £2bn.'

Technology and forecasting skills have improved so much. In my first job in Scotland, over twenty years ago, there were no radars and the first six months I was there was the wettest on record.

Darren Bett, weather presenter

The naming of the storms

Doris, Barbara and Frank might sound like a harmless group of pals on a night out at the bingo but, in weather terms, this trio was capable of doing serious damage. They are among the monikers given to winter storms in the UK and Ireland since the Met Office and its Irish counterpart Met Eireann first began their naming system, with a little help from social media, in 2015. The public were asked to come up with suitable names for each letter of the alphabet – excluding the tricky Q, U, X, Y and Z – and the resulting suggestions included traditional English names such as Desmond, Henry and Abigail along with the more Irish Clodagh and Orla.

The idea may have seemed whimsical but there was a serious reason to dub a severe storm Gertrude or Vernon. Analysts had discovered that the general public are more likely to be aware of a coming storm if it carries a human name and that more people will track its progress and take precautions to protect homes, businesses and their own selves from possible harm. It also makes it easier for people to share stories and discuss the storm on social media.

Last but not least, the new system cleared up confusion for weather presenters, who often came up with their own names such as the St Jude's Storm of 2013, so-called because it arrived on St Jude's Day, 28 October.

During the initial #nameourstorms campaign, the Met Office and Met Eireann received 10,000 suggestions from the public. These were kept and, each year, the two departments choose the most popular suggestions, taking care not to use names previously associated with well-known deadly storms such as Katrina.

At its launch, in 2015, Derrick Ryall, head of the Public Weather Service at the Met Office, said: 'We have seen how naming storms elsewhere in the world raises awareness of severe weather before it strikes. We hope that naming storms in line with the official severe weather warnings here will do the same and ensure everyone can keep themselves, their property and businesses safe and protected at times of severe weather.'

When is a storm named?

A storm is allocated a name when the National Severe Weather Warnings Service decides that the weather conditions have the potential to cause damage and disrupt lives. If a storm is likely to reach the warning levels of amber (be prepared) or red (take action) it will be named.

As well as severe gales, snow and rain can be considered, specifically deluges that could cause flooding as advised by the joint Environment Agency and Met Office Flood forecasting Centre for England and Wales, and jointly with SEPA for Scotland, issuing flood warnings.

Storm names 2015–2016

Abigail	Barney	Clodagh	Desmond	Eva	Frank	Gertrude
Henry	Imogen	Jake	Katie	Lawrence	Mary	Nigel
Orla	Phil	Rhonda	Steve	Tegan	Vernon	Wendy

Storm names 2016–2017

Angus	Barbara	Conor	Doris	Ewan	Fleur	Gabriel
Holly	Ivor	Jacqui	Kamil	Louise	Malcolm	Natalie
Oisín	Penelope	Robert	Susan	Thomas	Valerie	Wilbert

Hurricane Names

The National Hurricane Center in the USA started naming Atlantic tropical storms in 1953, and the lists are now presided over by an international committee at the

World Meteorological Organization (WMO). There are six lists of names which are repeated in rotation so, for example, Arlene was the first storm of the 2011 season and the 2017 season. Another six lists are used for naming hurricanes in the North Pacific.

The only time a name is changed is when a storm results in a disaster, such as the devastation wreaked by Hurricane Katrina in 2005. Then a new name is chosen at an annual WMO meeting. If more than twenty-one storms occur in a season, the Greek alphabet is used to name subsequent events.

If a hurricane or storm moves across the Atlantic to the British Isles it keeps its US name to avoid confusion but becomes 'Ex-hurricane X'.

WEATHER GIRLS

Initially hurricanes were only given girls' names as the men who formed the meteorological community in the USA thought something as wild, unpredictable and dangerous as a storm should naturally be female. But, in the 1970s, women began to join their ranks and protest at the slur. The first female US Secretary of Commerce, Juanita Kreps, agreed: in 1978, she ordered the NOAA (National Oceanic and Atmospheric Administration) to stop using women's names exclusively. At the first meeting of the newly formed WMO Hurricane Committee, a proposal to alternate between male and female names was agreed. Some Spanish and French names were also added to reflect the cultures of the countries in the Atlantic.

CHAPTER 7

The Shipping Forecast

It's part of the fabric of this intangible thing called
Britishness. Just like red telephone boxes, Wimbledon, the
chimes of Big Ben, the smell of cut grass, scones and jam.

Zeb Soanes, Radio 4 announcer

Although a direct descendant of Admiral FitzRoy's life-saving gale warnings, the Shipping Forecast as we know it today started life in 1921 at a wireless station in Poldhu, on the coast of Cornwall.

In 1924, the Air Ministry decided to expand it to a national service, provided from a transmitter in London, and some of the modern areas names – including Dogger, Forties, Wight and Shannon – were heard for the first time. A year later, in order to help sailors who didn't have the right equipment on board to pick up the signal,

the forecast was picked up by the BBC. It was put out on Long Wave, the best frequency to reach those at sea around the British Isles, and broadcast twice a day from the station at Daventry in Northamptonshire.

After a break for the Second World War, the Shipping Forecast returned in 1949 and the area covered expanded, taking the predictions out towards the Bay of Biscay in Spain and the coasts of Iceland and Norway. The thirteen named areas became twenty-six, and some familiar names – such as Rockall, Fastnet, Malin and Finisterre – were added. Orkney and Shetland became one area, now known as Fair Isle. Seven years later, the North Sea areas of

Forties and Dogger were cut down to make way for Viking and Fisher and, in 1984, three of the resulting areas were squeezed again to accommodate North and South Utsire.

The forecast's post-war return saw it first placed on the Light Programme – later known as Radio 2 – where it remained until 22 November 1978. It then switched to Radio 4, where it has been read four times a day ever since – at 00.48, 05.20, 12.01 and 17.54 – either on Long Wave only or on both LW and FM. Timing is crucial in the delivery of the familiar rhythmic incantation and the script must be a maximum of 370 words, apart from the final, longer forecast.

Over the last century, the Shipping Forecast has become a British institution with millions of devoted fans, many of whom have no maritime connection at all. Radio 4 listeners enjoy the lilting poetry of the daily bulletins, and many have claimed the late-night broadcast is perfect for lulling them off to sleep. In fact it is so engrained in the British way of life that plans to move one of the broadcasts by twelve minutes in 1995 sparked a national outcry and a debate in Parliament. A listeners' campaign group claimed the BBC had 'totally lost sight of the concept of public service broadcasting'. The plans were quietly shelved.

'SAFER LIVES, SAFER SHIPS, CLEANER SEAS'

The Shipping Forecast is actually the responsibility of a government department, the Maritime and Coastguard Agency. Under the UN Safety of Life at Sea (SOLAS) Convention 1974, the MCA has a legal obligation to provide critical weather and warning information to shipping around the UK. In order to fulfil this task, the agency – motto 'Safer Lives, Safer Ships, Cleaner Seas' – produces numerous daily forecasts, including the Shipping Forecast, through its UK Marine Weather Service, powered by the Met Office.

Andrew Colenutt, Hydrography and Meteorology Manager at the MCA says: 'The affection for and relationship with the Shipping Forecast has continued to grow, welding itself into the national psyche, resulting in the Shipping Forecast becoming a much treasured institution.'

IT'S SIMPLY NOT CRICKET

The Shipping Forecast found itself on a sticky wicket when it clashed with another beloved British institution in January 2011. England were on the verge of winning the Ashes for the first time in twenty-four years when the

Radio 4 broadcast switched to its customary post-midnight warnings, leaving cricket fans incensed.

While the announcer toured Dogger, Cromarty and German Bight, Australia's final batsman Michael Beer had been bowled by England's Chris Tremlett and victory celebrations were under way.

One furious sports fan tweeted: 'Was an Aussie responsible for scheduling the cricket forecast?' But some supported the Radio 4 decision, with one pointing out: 'Cricket is cricket but the shipping forecast saves lives.'

It was in fact the third time the unfortunate timing had led to the final wickets being missed in that series, during the second test in Adelaide and the fourth test in Melbourne.

When I was a boy I would record the Shipping Forecast on my cassette recorder and then type it out so I could pretend to read it out like they do on Radio 4.

Who knew I would one day do it for real! It's my favourite part of the job.

Nick Miller, weather presenter

WHAT'S IN A NAME?

The thirty-one regions are read out in strict order starting with Viking and moving round Britain in a clockwise direction. The fascinating names are part of the charm of the bulletin and, while all but one – FitzRoy – are named after geographical features, each has its own story to tell.

Here's our whistle-stop tour of the Shipping Forecast regions.

Viking

One of the six names to come directly from a sandbank in the area, along with Forties, Dogger, Fisher, Sole and Bailey. The bank, in the North Sea off the coast of Scotland, gets its name from the marauding Nordic warriors from days of yore whose fat-bottomed boats gave them a tactical advantage and saw them ruling the waves in these parts from the eighth century to the eleventh.

North Utsire and South Utsire

Although it boasts two regions in the list, Utsira, just off the coast of Norway, is only one island. It's tiny – just 10 km² – and has a population of just 240. Although it has been spelt Utsira since 1925, the BBC are still using the ancient spelling.

Forties

Maritime charts detail the depth of the sea in fathoms, to help sailors steer clear of shallow waters. On such a map, to the north of Aberdeen, is a large areas of '40s', indicating a plateau which is 40 fathoms below sea which has been named the Long Forties. That, in turn, gave its name to the shipping region.

Cromarty

Named after the Cromarty Firth, an inlet on the Scottish coast, and the village of Cromarty, once a thriving fishing port in the Highlands. The name comes from the Gaelic word *crom*, meaning 'crooked', and *bati*, meaning 'bay'.

Tyne

Named after the Tyne estuary, where the River Tyne meets the North Sea, this area was once home to a huge ship-building industry which has since died out.

Dogger

Named after the Dogger Bank, which was once a small tundra inhabited by mammoths, lions and rhinoceros, now called Doggerland. A tsunami in around 600 BC wiped out the wildlife and turned it into a sandbank. The name Dogger comes from a type of shallow Dutch fishing vessel used to catch cod.

Fisher

Also named after a sandbank, which consists of the Great Fisher Bank and Little Fisher Bank, it is an area in the North Sea, just off Denmark.

GERMAN BIGHT

When the Shipping Forecast returned, four years after the Second World War, one of the areas chosen by the British was rather tactlessly labelled Heligoland. This was a sore point with the defeated Germans, who had seen the island of the same name bombarded by British bombs and, as recently as 1947, the Royal Navy had caused a massive explosion in order to destroy the U-Boat pens there. In 1956, the name was changed to German Bight, after an indentation in the North Sea coast between Germany and Denmark.

Humber

Named after the estuary on the east coast of Northern England, Humber originally stretched from Great Yarmouth to Scotland, but now covers the area between the Norfolk Coast and the Hook of Holland.

Thames

Another estuary lends its name to Thames, one of the original areas from the 1924 broadcasts.

Dover

Named after the Kentish town which in turn gives its name to the Strait of Dover in the English Channel, which is one of the busiest stretches of water in the world, used by over 400 commercial vessels a day.

Wight

The area around the Isle of Wight is one of the warmest places in the UK but with steady head winds, meaning it has become the heart of the UK yachting scene. The annual Cowes Week, established in 1826, is the most popular regatta in the world with 1,000 boats and 8,000 competitors taking part each year.

Portland

Portland is an island off the coast of Dorset which measures 6 km by 2.7 km and has a population of 12,400. Its port is one of the largest manmade harbours in the world and served as a Royal Naval base between 1905 and 1995.

Plymouth

Named after the Devon seafaring city famous for being the starting point for the Pilgrim Fathers, who set off for a new life in the Americas in 1620, and for Plymouth Hoe, where Sir Francis Drake insisted on finishing his

game of bowls before taking on the Spanish Armada
in 1588.

Biscay

The Bay of Biscay, which gives this region its moniker, is
a large gulf in the Atlantic that runs along the coasts of
France and Spain. Biscay has maintained its boundaries
since 1949.

Trafalgar

Oddly enough, the area covered by Trafalgar does *not*
include Spain's Cape Trafalgar or the site of Admiral
Nelson's famous battle against Napoleon in 1805. Instead,
it takes in much of Portugal. Another curious fact is that
Trafalgar is only included in the longer bulletin, at 00.48
hours, unless there is a gale warning in its area.

FITZROY – LOSING ITS IDENTITY

In 2002, there was a public outcry when the Met Office
announced that Finisterre was to be renamed FitzRoy
in honour of its esteemed founder, Admiral FitzRoy. The
decision didn't come completely out of the blue, so to
speak, but was taken because the Spanish forecasts used

Finisterre for a smaller area and the United Nations World Meteorological Organization decreed that this was causing confusion.

The British public were furious, with letters being fired off to *The Times*, the BBC and the Met Office, but the change went ahead regardless.

Incidentally, Finisterre came from the Latin meaning 'the end of the Earth' and harked back to the days when sailors believed the world was flat and that if they sailed as far as this area, they would fall off.

Sole

One of only six of the Shipping Forecast areas to have no mainland boundary, Sole is named after two sandbanks – the Great Sole Bank and Little Sole Bank. It stretches to the Scilly Isles in the east and, with warm Gulf Stream waters, is a perfect feeding ground for fish, including sole.

Lundy

Named after the largest island in the Bristol Channel, off the coast of Devon, which has a population of just twenty-eight people. Just three miles long, the island was bought by the National Trust in 1969 but previous inhabitants have included Barbary Pirates, Knights Templar and, in the English Civil War, Royalist Thomas Bushell, who held the island for King Charles I until 1647.

FASTNET

Many will associate the title with the famous yacht race which takes place every two years with a course from Cowes, round the Fastnet Rock off the coast of Ireland and back to Plymouth – a total of 608 nautical miles (1,126 km). In August 1979, gale warnings issued in the Shipping Forecast as the 306 yachts set off predicted 'south-westerly winds, force 4 to 5 increasing to force 6 to 7 for a time'. Two days later, the Met Office warned of gale force 10 wind as a depression formed over the Atlantic, and disaster struck. Over the next two days five boats sank, 100 were knocked down and 77 rolled. During a huge rescue effort, involving RAF helicopters and ships and a Dutch warship, 125 yachtsmen were plucked from the sea but 18 people – 15 sailors and three rescuers – lost their lives.

Irish Sea

Stretching from the west coast of Wales up to the Scottish border and across to the east coast of Ireland, the Irish Sea region covers the once-thriving shipbuilding cities of Liverpool and Belfast, as well as the Irish capital of Dublin.

Shannon

The longest river in Ireland, the River Shannon, lends its name to this area and is itself named after Sionna, a Celtic goddess. Legend has it that she was originally a mortal woman who searched for the Well of Knowledge, known as Connla's Well, guarded by the water god Nechtan and his servants. When Sionna approached the well and opened the cover, the water rose up and carried her to the sea, resulting in the river that bears her name.

Rockall

The most inhospitable of the sea areas, having virtually no habitable land, Rockall stretches from the tip of Ireland 300 miles north towards Iceland. The jagged rock after which it is named is one of three long since dormant volcano peaks – the other two being Hasselwood Rock and Helen's Peak. Rockall experiences the highest waves recorded in any shipping area – at 29 metres (95 feet).

Malin

Malin Head, in County Donegal, boasts the most northerly point in Ireland, Banba's Crown – named after the patron goddess of the country. Malin Head also has one of the twenty-two weather stations used to collate the Shipping Forecast.

Hebrides

The Inner and Outer Hebrides is an archipelago off the west coast of Scotland which includes such islands as Lewis, Mull, Colonsay and Skye. The Inner Hebrides are made up of thirty-five inhabited islands as well as forty-four uninhabited islands with an area greater than seventy-four acres, while the Outer Hebrides has fifteen inhabited islands and more than fifty uninhabited. The Shipping Forecast is of huge interest to the 46,000 islanders as the majority rely on boats and ferries to deliver goods and to come and go from the islands.

Bailey

Named after a sandbank in the North Atlantic, between Scotland and Ireland, Bailey is all sea and has no land whatsoever. The wrecks of at least seven German U-boats, sunk by British forces in the Second World War, litter the seabed there.

Fair Isle

The merging of Orkney and Shetland into one area in 1949 presented the Met Office with a dilemma over the name – so they chose to call it after a third island, which sits halfway between the two. The tiny Scottish island, with a population of just fifty-five, is more famous for its distinctive knitted sweaters.

Faeroes

Originally known as 'Faroes' in the forecast, the spelling was corrected in 1949 to match the Faeroe Islands from whence its name originates. Legend has it that these rocky isles off the north coast of Scotland were created when God cleaned out his finger nails after creating the Earth. The name comes from the old Norse word *faer*, meaning 'sheep', and the islands are an autonomous region within the Danish realm. Their position, in the path of depressions moving north-east, means heavy rain and gales are common at all times of the year.

Southeast Iceland

With one of the longest coastlines of any forecast area, this is also the coldest and stormiest. In fact, it is the only area to get regular mentions of 'icing' – when strong winds and a cold sea combine to meaning spray hitting the ship immediately freezes.

My favourite is 'light icing'. I love saying that – it makes me think of cakes.

Kathy Clugston, BBC radio announcer

THE OUTLOOK IS FAIR

One nautical family paid tribute to the role of the Shipping Forecast in their lives – by naming their children after the sea areas. South Tyneside mum Stephanie Waring and her ship's captain husband Andrew called their first child Shannon in 1990. Her sister Khadine Doyle, and husband Kevin, followed by calling their son Bailey and Stephanie's second daughter was then named Tyne.

Khadine told the *Sunderland Echo*: 'I'm not going to have any more children, and neither is Stephanie. Besides, there are no nice names left.'

The Shipping Forecast was one of the subjects I received the most letters about, although not all of them were complimentary. One reader accused me of mispronouncing the word 'shipping' – putting 'tt' where 'pp' should have been. He even threatened to write to the controller of Radio 4 in disgust at my use of bad language.

Charlotte Green, Radio 4 announcer

SHIPPING OFF

The Shipping Forecast on Radio 4 is so well-timed you could set your clock by it, so it's not surprising that its fans were all at sea when, on 30 May 2014, for the first time in ninety years, Radio 4 failed to broadcast the 05.20 bulletin. A technical issue meant that, although the BBC announcer was reading it out loud, it was broadcast on the BBC World Service instead.

A Radio 4 spokesperson explained: 'Unfortunately our usual switch from BBC World Service, which is broadcast on Radio 4 overnight, didn't go as planned and was delayed by around twenty minutes.'

Fans took to Twitter to record their dismay at this unexpected start to the day with one tweeting: 'I'm all out of sync today. No shipping forecast on @BBCRadio4 didn't help. I didn't know where I was!' Another slightly more worried soul tweeted: 'No shipping forecast? If UK submarines don't get shipping forecast, don't they launch nuclear attack?'

The latter refers to an urban myth that commanders of the Royal Navy's nuclear submarines are required to listen out for Radio 4 on Long Wave if they think the UK is under nuclear attack. Luckily, a source at the Royal Navy revealed this is not true. They also told *The Independent*: 'UK Submarines have a number of ways to gather meteorological data and they are certainly not dependent on the Shipping Forecast for their information.'

THE MUSIC OF THE SEA

Before the poetic tones of the nightly Shipping Forecast, at 00.48 hours, come the mellifluous sounds of 'Sailing By'. The familiar tune was originally intended as a filler as the midnight news didn't always end at a precise time. However, it served a dual purpose, allowing sailors to locate the correct Long Wave channel as they waited for the late-night update on conditions.

The tune is performed by the Alan Perry/ William Gardner Orchestra, credited as the Perry Gardner Orchestra on BBC recordings, but that's not the whole story. In fact, Alan Perry and William Gardner are pseudonyms for the tune's composers Ernest Tomlinson and Peter Hope.

The tune is much loved by listeners – including some famous names. In 2004, Pulp singer Jarvis Cocker chose it as one of his eight tracks on *Desert Island Discs*. He explained: 'For many years I used it as an aid for restful sleep. I find something very comforting about listening to it when you're laid in bed.' He also felt it would give him hope, as he sat on the mythical Desert Island, that a ship might sail by and rescue him. He added: 'This would be something that could help me with the isolation.'

*We love tradition and history, and the Shipping Forecast
is just that. I've heard recently though that despite
new technology, fishermen still put their trust in the
Shipping Forecast.*

*I love presenting it. It's the only scripted piece we do and
it's nine minutes long. You're supposed to come out to the
second and hand back to the news presenter and I become
obsessed about coming out on time. I get really frustrated
if I'm a few seconds over or under.*

Louise Lear, weather presenter

THE SHIPPING FORECAST IN POPULAR CULTURE

The poetry of the broadcasts has inspired many in their own tributes to this national institution. The Blur song 'This Is A Low' contains several references to the forecast with mentions of Biscay, Dogger, Thames, Tyne, Forth, Cromarty, Forties and Malin. In his autobiography *A Bit of a Blur*, bassist Alex James revealed that the 1995 *Parklife* track started as an instrumental, called 'We Are The Low', as lead singer Damon Albarn was struggling with lyrics. He went on: 'For Christmas I bought him a handkerchief with a map of the shipping forecast regions on it ... you can never tell where the muse is going to appear.'

Alex added: 'We always found the shipping forecast soothing. We used to listen to it [on tour] to remind us of home. It's very good for a hangover. Good cure for insomnia, too.' With recording time running out, Damon looked to the hanky for inspiration and came up with several lines: 'Around the Bay of Biscay and back for tea'; 'Hit traffic on the Dogger Bank / Up the Thames to find a taxi rank'; 'Up the Tyne, Forth and Cromarty, there's a low in the High Forties'; and 'on the Malin Head, Blackpool looks blue and red.'

Radiohead's Thom Yorke took similar inspiration for the track 'In Limbo', on the 2000 album *Kid A*, which begins 'Lundy, Fastnet, Irish Sea, I got a message I can't read.'

Poets have also found inspiration in the words, with Seamus Heaney writing a sonnet entitled 'The Shipping Forecast', while Poet Laureate Carol Ann Duffy's 'Prayer' ends with the haunting lines:

> *Darkness outside. Inside, the radio's prayer –*
>
> *Rockall. Malin. Dogger. Finisterre.*

SPECIAL GUEST

Politician John Prescott ended up as a guest announcer in 2011 after tweeting that he was in the studio for *The World Tonight* and joking that it was so late he might as well stay on and do the Shipping Forecast. Presenter Alice Arnold quickly replied saying he was welcome to give it a go, as she fancied an early night. John valiantly took up the offer and broadcast his forecast for Red Nose Day.

GOING FOR GOLD

Danny Boyle's celebration of all things British at the opening ceremony of the 2012 Olympics in London, would not have been complete without a tribute to the Shipping Forecast. In fact, a recitation kicked off the ceremony, playing over Elgar's 'Nimrod' to represent Britain's maritime heritage.

This wasn't the first time it had featured at the games. Four years earlier, for the Beijing Olympics, composer Philip Shepard was looking for ways to sum up Britishness and the 'island mentality' for the closing ceremony. He decided to include a nod to the broadcasts, particularly the areas of North Utsire, South Utsire and Lundy, Fastnet, Irish Sea, and asked BBC announcer Zeb Soanes to repeat them.

'He liked the mantra-like way that the words and locations flowed,' Zeb told BBC News. 'I recorded them over the soundtrack whilst listening to the music in my headphones.' He also recorded the World Service call sign, 'This is London', as an opener to the music, and the iconic tube warning, 'Mind the gap.'

The music and announcements provided the backdrop to the eight-minute show representing the handover of the Olympic torch to London, which also featured a classic red double decker bus and appearances from David Beckham and Leona Lewis.

When I first started at BBC Weather, I had a lot of training on how to effectively broadcast the weather using my knowledge of meteorology. The Shipping Forecast was one area where 'getting it right' really matters as it is such a specialist broadcast with its own quirks and ways of doing things. When I did my first Shipping Forecast after a long night shift, the nerves got the better of me and I said, 'Good morning, and now the Shopping *Forecast,' quickly correcting myself but the damage was done.*

While I didn't think it was funny at the time, my colleagues (and now I) thought it was hilarious.

Simon King, weather presenter

WHAT DOES IT ALL MEAN?

Lovers of the Shipping Forecast are lulled by the sound of familiar terms, such as 'Sea state, slight', 'Veering north-westerly' and 'Becoming cyclonic'. But while the landlubbers might not get the significance of each term, for those in peril on the sea they provide precise information.

GLOSSARY OF TERMS

Gale warnings

Gale	Winds of at least Beaufort force 8 (34–40 knots) or gusts reaching 43–51 knots
Severe gale	Winds of force 9 (41–47 knots) or gusts reaching 52–60 knots
Storm	Winds of force 10 (48–55 knots) or gusts reaching 61–68 knots
Violent storm	Winds of force 11 (56–63 knots) or gusts of 69 knots or more
Hurricane force	Winds of force 12 (64 knots or more). 'Hurricane force' is used rather than 'hurricane', which means a tropical cyclone, not experienced in British waters.

Time Scale

Imminent   Expected within 6 hours of time of issue

Soon   Expected within 6–12 hours

Later   Expected after more than 12 hours

Visibility

Very poor   Less than 1,000 metres

Poor   Between 1,000 metres and 2 nautical miles

Moderate   Between 2 and 5 nautical miles

Good   More than 5 nautical miles

Movement of pressure systems

Slowly   Moving at less than 15 knots

Steadily   Moving at 15–25 knots

Rather quickly   Moving at 25–35 knots

Rapidly   Moving at 35–45 knots

Very rapidly   Moving at more than 45 knots

Wind

Becoming cyclonic   Indicates a considerable change in wind direction across the path of a depression within the forecast area

Veering	The changing of the wind direction clockwise, e.g. SW to W
Backing	The changing of the wind anticlockwise, e.g. SE to NE

Sea state

Smooth	Wave height less than 0.5 m
Slight	Wave height of 0.5 to 1.25 m
Moderate	Wave height of 1.25 to 2.5 m
Rough	Wave height of 2.5 to 4.0 m
Very rough	Wave height of 4.0 to 6.0 m
High	Wave height of 6.0 to 9.0 m
Very high	Wave height of 9.0 to 14.0 m
Phenomenal	Wave height more than 14.0 m

I think it's comforting to people who don't understand the forecast, who are lying in bed, imagining these boats being tossed around in the sea, and snuggle down feeling glad to be in bed.

Zeb Soanes, Radio 4 announcer

CHAPTER 8

A World of Weather Folklore

The wonders of weather have inspired legends and superstitions since time began. From Roman and Greek mythology, to tribal ritual in Africa, the changing seasons and unpredictable elements are behind stories passed down through countless generations and festivals that still take place today.

Here's a whirlwind tour of the world's weather folklore.

THE USA

Groundhog Day

Made famous in a classic film comedy starring Bill Murray as a weatherman trapped in an endlessly recurring 24-hour cycle, Groundhog Day is an ancient tradition that still survives today in many parts of the USA. On 2 February, locals gather to watch a groundhog emerge from its burrow and, according to folklore, if it is cloudy the spring season is about to start but if it is sunny enough for the animal to see its shadow the harsh winter weather will carry on for another six weeks. The biggest celebration of the day is in Punxsutawney, Pennsylvania, where the 1993 film was set and where the legendary groundhog Punxsutawney Phil emerges from his hole on Gobbler's Knob to an audience of hundreds.

This quaint tradition actually originated in medieval Germany, where the shadow of a badger was used to reveal whether or not spring was on its way. German immigrants brought this tradition to the USA, where it became a groundhog, which is also known as the 'thickwood badger'.

The Woollybear Festival

While Punxsutawney Phil is called on to herald the spring, another creature is celebrated for its weather prediction skills, 200 miles away in Vermilion, Ohio. When the woolly bear caterpillars hatch from their eggs in the autumn, the ratio of black versus orange on the new batch's stripes is said to indicate the severity of the coming winter. The blacker the bristles the worse the winter will be.

This folklore has now become the centre of an annual festival, held on a Sunday around 1 October. It was the brainchild of Cleveland TV weatherman Dick Goddard and, since its humble beginnings in 1972, has grown into a major attraction attended by over 100,000 people. The celebration includes a long parade with floats and marching bands and an event called the Woolly Bear 500, which kicks off with the Chief of Police and the Chief of Fire choosing caterpillars to race against each other.

A similar festival is held in North Carolina and is named the Woolly Worm Festival, after the alternative names for the same creature.

MANHATTANHENGE

As many a tourist will know, the streets of New York City are designed on a grid system, set out in a plan in 1811, with the parallel streets lying perpendicular to the avenues. But the grid's angle, lying 29 degrees clockwise for east-west, means that twice a year a stunning solar spectacle occurs.

On 28 May and 12 July, the sun aligns with the grid and sets at the end of the Manhattan streets, so that it looks like a huge ball of fire nestling between the tall, straight-sided building. As it happens, the two dates coincide with Memorial Day and Baseball's All Star break, both big celebrations in the US calendar, and thousands flock to the city to watch the spectacular sunset. The phenomenon has been compared to the Summer and Winter Solstice at Stonehenge, hence the name.

For the best view, experts suggest standing as far east in Manhattan as possible, looking west, and the best streets are said to be 14th, 23rd, 34th, 42nd and 57th.

EUROPE

Snow Burn

The end of winter is celebrated in explosive style in Switzerland, where a spring festival called the Sechseläuten ends with the burning of a snowman figure, known as the Böögg. The effigy – whose name is related to the 'boogeyman' of popular folklore – is packed with explosives and thrown on a fire.

The rate at which it burns is said to predict the sort of summer ahead: the faster it is consumed by the flames, the better the weather will be. If it explodes in ten minutes, the summer will be dry and sunny and an explosion after ten means a wet summer.

Festival of Fire

The spring celebration in Valencia, Spain, attracts over three million tourists every year. The Fallas (or Falles) is a week-long event which sees festival-goers dressing up in medieval costume and celebrating in the streets. It kicks off with a parade of colourful floats in honour of Saint Joseph and ends with the burning of *ninots*, satirical papier-mâché figurines stuffed with firecrackers.

Grandma March

In Bulgarian folklore, Baba Marta is an old woman who is said to usher in the warm weather of spring. There are many different myths around Baba Marta – which translates as Grandmother March – but the last snow of the winter is said to be down to her shaking out her mattress while spring cleaning. One story is that she has fallen out with her brothers, January and February, and that her smile makes the spring sun shine.

Bulgarians celebrate the feisty old woman with a holiday on 1 March, known as Baba Marta Day, and they exchange red and white bands called *martenitsi*, which symbolise health and happiness.

A Watery Grave

The people of Poland celebrate the first day of spring with an age-old tradition which involves drowning a doll in the river. The straw effigy, known as a Marzanna, represents the cold, gloomy winter and, after marching her through the streets, the locals throw her into a river or lake to represent the death of the harshest season.

Russian Rainmaker

In a village near Dorpat in Russia, a special ritual to encourage rain was observed up to the nineteenth century. If a dry spell was threatening crops, three men would climb a tree to be nearer the heavens and each perform their own role. The first would bang on a kettle or pot to imitate thunder, the second would rub two firebrands together to produce a spark, representing lightning, and a third, known as 'the rainmaker' poured water over a bunch of twigs to imitate a much-needed downpour.

ASIA

Moon on a Plate

Many Chinese customs are heavily linked to the moon and the sun and in Li-Ji, an ancient book of ceremonies, it states that the Emperor should offer a sacrifice to the moon in autumn and the sun in spring. The Chinese calendar is based on the lunar cycle and one of the customs still practised today is the baking, eating and sharing of mooncakes to celebrate the birthday of the moon, in the eighth lunar month.

Although there are regional variations, the basic cakes are circular pastry cases containing a sweet heavy filling and will traditionally contain a whole egg yolk, to represent the moon.

Legend has it that the Ming revolutionaries overthrew Mongol rulers in the fourteenth century by using secret messages hidden inside mooncakes. It is said that the leaders spread rumours of a deadly plague which could only be prevented by eating a special mooncake. In the subsequent rush to eat these magical delicacies, notes coordinating the Han Chinese revolt on the fifteenth day of the eighth lunar month were surreptitiously distributed. The cakes are now a central part of the Mid-Autumn Festival, which is celebrated on that date every year.

Coldblooded Killer

On snowy nights, according to Japanese folk tales, a tall, strikingly beautiful woman with black hair and blue lips appears to travellers. She is Yuki-onna, the Snow Woman, who glides across the snow leaving no prints and strikes fear into the hearts of men. She seeks out those trapped in a snowstorm and sends them to sleep, and certain death, with her icy breath.

In some legends, Yuki-onna comes knocking at the door in the form of a blizzard and takes the lives of the sleeping residents inside. In others, she uses her beauty to seduce weak-willed men before sucking the lifeblood from them.

In one popular story, Yuki-onna spared the life of a young, handsome man on his promise he would keep her a secret. Years later, the man met a beautiful woman, married her and had children. But when he finally revealed the secret of his escape to his wife, she revealed herself as the Snow Woman in disguise. For the sake of her children, however, she spares him a second time.

The Selfless Hare

Ancient Indians believed that there was a silhouette of a hare on the moon. The story went that the god of the sky, Indra, wanted to test the generosity of a hare, who had offered his own body as a sacrifice to the gods. Indra disguised himself as a hungry beggar and lit a fire on which the willing hare then offered to roast its own meat, before shaking off insects from his fur and climbing in.

Indra was so impressed with this selfless act that he imprinted the hare's shadow on the moon as a reminder to all below.

Drought Dragons and Rain Gods

Indian mythology suggested that long periods of drought were caused by a malevolent dragon which prevented the rain from falling to the ground. Ancient Indians prayed to the storm god to distract the dragon so that he would allow the rain to come.

Today some Indians maintain bizarre rituals to encourage the rain gods to favour their farmland. In recent years, it has been reported that drought-hit farms in Bihar are sometimes ploughed by naked, unmarried girls in a ritual to encourage rain. The theory is that the act will embarrass the gods into sending the much-needed downpour and rescuing the crops.

A Sunny Spell

A belief in witchcraft and magic is still widespread in Indonesia and the use of *dukuns*, or shamans, is common. One popular figure in Indonesian society is the *pawang hujan*, or rain shaman, who is thought to have powers of control over weather and is frequently hired to keep the downpours at bay in the country's rainy season.

Their services are seen as a necessary expense for anyone planning a big event and the belief in their effectiveness goes to the highest level in the government. After four dry days at a recent four-day Interpol conference, held in Bali, National Police Chief Tito Karnavian stood up to make a speech and told attendees: 'This place is a genuine paradise. Our rain shaman's got everything handled for you.'

AFRICA

The rich tradition of African folklore often attributes bad weather to monstrous deities and evil spirits, who cause storms, send bolts of lightning to punish wrongdoing and withhold much-needed rain. Many tribes traditionally believed that evil spirits inhabited whirlwinds and they would attempt to fight the wind with long knives, in a bid to see the spirit off. In Kenya, the god of thunder, Mkunga Mburu, is said to roam the heavens on a huge black bull throwing spears at clouds to make the thunderclaps.

Storm Serpent

In South African legend, a mythical creature called the Inkanyamba controls the weather. It is said to be a huge carnivorous eel-like animal with massive fins and a horse-shaped head. It lived in the waterfalls and lakes of the country's forests and if it was angered, its wrath would create severe summer storms.

The legend is undoubtedly inspired by the huge eels that live in the lakes and can grow up to 1.6 metres (6 feet) long.

Seasonal Sacrifice

Yorubaland, which covers much of modern-day Nigeria and parts of Benin, has a tradition of rainmaking rituals stretching back through the centuries. Although the country has a prolonged wet season, and abundant fruitfulness, crops can suffer if the dry season, between November and April, is entirely devoid of rain.

If this happened, the rainmaker was called upon to dance and chant around a boiling pot. If the heavens didn't open in the following weeks, a state of emergency was declared, and domestic animals were slaughtered as a sacrifice to the goddess who presided over the rainy season.

Today, many Yoruban people still celebrate the arrival of the rainy season with a huge festival, dancing and feasting and, in some cases, a sacrifice is still made to the rain gods.

The Rain Queen

The Rain Queen, or Modjadji, is a revered position to the Lovedu people of South Africa's Limpopo region and is a fundamental part of their culture. The human embodiment of the rain goddess, she is believed to have magical rainmaking powers and, as well as being able to keep the land watered, she is said to send storms to the enemy of her people.

The legend stretches back to the sixteenth century, when Dzugundini, the daughter of a chief, fled her village after being impregnated by her own brother, stealing the chief's rainmaking skills. She established a new tribe. Some years later, the tribe's leader, Mugodo, warned of a family plot against him, murdered all his sons and married his own daughter, living with her in a secret forest retreat. Her first daughter, Modjadji, became Rain Queen when Mugodo died but stayed in the forest, casting spells to keep the rain falling. In periods of drought, many other tribes sent messengers to ask her to help them summon rain and even Shaka, the Zulu warrior king, sent emissaries to seek her blessings.

The title was then passed down through the matriarchal line and came with a strict set of rules. Rain Queens were supposed to remain unmarried and any partners were chosen by the Royal Counsel, and had to be in perfect health at all time, so were expected to commit suicide at the first sign of serious illness, or at the age of 60.

The post has not been held by anyone since 2005, when Queen Modjadji VI died at the age of 27, leaving only a male heir.

SOUTH AMERICA

Wild Woman of the Woods

While wandering in the woods in Colombia, it pays to stay on the path or you could end up facing the wrath of La Mardemonte (Mother Mountain). The legendary spirit is portrayed as a large, curvy woman with big teeth and protruding eyes, dressed in clothes made from moss.

Rarely seen, but often heard in the form of a haunting wailing sound coming from the forest at night, she is said to control the weather and use it to punish any human who causes damage to nature.

Snakes in the Sky

A bird-chomping snake is responsible for long dry spells according to the folklore of the Nivaklé people, of Paraguay. Tsamtás serpents live in the middle of the sky and radiate heat, causing temperatures to rise. They are also blamed for stopping and eating the Fanxás or thunderbirds who fly from the south and bring rain and can only be defeated by shamans tearing down their nests.

Written in the Stars

When Peruvians want to predict the rainfall during the growing season, they look to the stars. The brightness of the Pleiades constellation at the time of the winter solstice is believed to indicate the amount of rain to come in the summer. The brighter the stars, the more rain will come and the planting of their main crop, potatoes, is timed accordingly.

This centuries-old forecasting method is not as way out as it sounds. Studies carried out by the University of California found that poor visibility of the Pleiades in June, caused by an increase in high cirrus clouds, indicates an El Niño year when the surface waters of the Pacific heat up. This event often means less rainfall in the coming months.

A BOLT FROM THE BLUE

The violence and majesty of lightning has fired the imagination and inspired myths on every continent and in every culture.

Ancient Greeks believed that lightning was a weapon of Zeus given to him as a reward for rescuing the three Cyclopes – Brontes, Steropes and Arges – from Hades. Thunder was said to be the one-eyed monsters working to forge the thunderbolts for Zeus, for him to cast down on mortals who had angered him. Any spot struck by lightning was regarded as sacred, and temples were often built on the sites to appease the angry gods.

In Roman mythology the bolts are cast down by Jupiter, god of the sky.

In Norse mythology, Thor, the son of Odin, makes the sparks with his mighty hammer, Mjölnir, as he rides across the sky in a noisy chariot.

Navajo Indians believed lightning came from the Thunderbird and depicted the bolts as a twinkle in the mythical bird's eye. It was said to have healing powers.

In Hinduism, the bolts are the domain of the storm gods known as Muratas, which number up to sixty. They are attendants of Indra, and said to be bad tempered and violent, with iron teeth, and golden weapons which are thrown down as lightning.

In Nigeria, the Yorubas believed that lightning was a magical storm spirit who scolded the tribesmen by spitting fiery bolts from his mouth and punished offences by destroying property or aiming his bolts at the perpetrator.

The lightning bird appears in the mythology of many African tribes, including the Bantu, Zulu, Pondo and Xhosa. Known as the impundulu or thekwane, this black and white bird, the size of a man, is said to bring thunder by flapping its wings and summon lightning from its talons. It is strongly associated with witchcraft, and is seen as a blood-sucking familiar to witches who can take the form of a young man to seduce women. The tufted umber, the bird known in South Africa as the hammerkop, is often seen as a manifestation of this creature and to destroy its nest is thought to bring storms.

Benjamin Franklin Drops a Clanger

Up until the eighteenth century, in both the USA and Europe, church steeples and spires were often the tallest buildings in any town and were the frequent victims of lightning strikes. Superstitious Christians believed that the 'evil spirits' behind the violent storms which wreaked so much damage could be warded off with loud noises, particularly the ringing of the church bells. In many churches the bells had inscriptions hailing their powers to ward off lightning and 'malignant demons', with a typical message reading 'It is I who dissipate the thunders'.

In 1749, after extensive research into electricity and why storms resulted in churches burning down, Benjamin Franklin concluded that with an iron rod 'the electrical fire would be drawn out of a cloud silently, before it could come near enough to strike'. He came up with the lightning rod or conductor, designed to harness the electricity and send it safely to earth without damaging the steeple.

Originally intended to be incorporated in the design of Christ Church in Philadelphia, which was under construction, Franklin tested his theory in 1752 at considerable personal risk, climbing to the top of the new church to experiment with conductive rods. He lived to tell the tale and similar experiments were soon being conducted all over Europe.

The church, however, was slow to drop its archaic practices in the face of this new scientific evidence. In 1768, Harvard Professor John Winthrop wrote to Franklin about the 'force of prejudice' which was preventing the church from adopting the rods. After reading about the destruction of the spire of St Bride's Church in London, he wrote: 'It is amazing to me that, after the full demonstrations you have given of the identity of lightning and electricity, and the power of metalline conductors, they should ever think of repairing that steeple without conductors.'

Franklin replied that he was not surprised that even learned men, 'hold out against new knowledge that does not square with their preconceptions'. Referring to the bell-ringing, he marvelled at 'how long men can retain practices that are conformable to their prejudices, and expect a benefit from those practices, though constant experience shows their inutility'.

The way I see it, if you want the rainbow, you gotta put up with the rain.

Dolly Parton

RAINBOWS

Like lightning, the beauty and rarity of a rainbow means it is bound to feature in folklore and superstition. For the Irish, it famously points the way to buried pots of gold (see box on pages 163–164), but for many it is a bridge to the heavens, for others a sign from the gods and for some it represents an evil spirit.

In Norse legend, the rainbow was a burning bridge called the Bifrost which connected earth with Asgard, home of the gods. Only heroes killed in battle were able to use it to ascend to the heavens. Similarly, the ancient Polynesians believed it was a ladder which their heroes climbed to reach heaven.

The ancient Japanese saw the rainbow as a bridge that worked the other way, allowing their deceased ancestors to come down to Earth. Maori folklore includes the story of the moon, Hina, who married a mortal and then constructed the rainbow so that he could return to Earth in his dying days, as death could not enter the homes of the immortals.

In Greek mythology, Iris, wife of the god Zephyrus and messenger to the gods, ran between Heaven and Earth to deliver her warning of war and retribution, always dressed in beautiful multi-coloured robes, creating a stunning rainbow as she ran. This myth inspired the word 'iridescent', meaning to display different colours that can change when viewed from different angles. Hawaiian legend has a similar character called the rainbow maiden, or Anuenue, who acts as a messenger to her divine brothers Tane and Kanaloa.

In the Bible, in the book of Genesis, the rainbow which appears after Noah's flood is a promise from God that he will never again cause such death and destruction.

Rainbows weren't always a good thing. Ancient Zulus believed rainbows were colourful snakes who came down to drink from the Earth's cool waters. But if they reached a pool the deadly serpents would stay there and devour anybody who entered the water. The ancient Karen people in Southeast Asia thought the rainbow was a demonic spirit who caused sudden deaths and consumed the souls of humans, leaving it so thirsty it would have to stretch down to the Earth to drink the water.

In Australian Aboriginal legend, the Rainbow Serpent is a huge, often evil snake which has different names from tribe to tribe.

There are various superstitions attached to rainbows too. In Bulgaria, it is said that anyone who walks under a rainbow will change gender and one anonymous proverb predicts that if your house is within the arch of a rainbow, disaster is on its way.

POTTY STORY

The Irish legend of the leprechaun hiding pots of gold at the end of a rainbow is well known and has inspired songs and even films, including the classic *Finian's Rainbow*, starring Fred Astaire, in 1968.

But the story behind the legend is not so famous. The story actually stretches back to the Viking invasion of the ninth century, when the looting, pillaging Scandinavians brought coins and treasures to the shores of the Emerald Isle. When they left, the Vikings were said to have appointed the mischievous little elves as guardians of the pots that they buried at locations dotted about the countryside.

The leprechauns then reburied the treasures deep in the ground, and the end of the rainbow was thought to point to the location of the pots. However, should anyone find the end of the rainbow, the leprechaun will try to distract the finder and then whip away the treasure.

CHAPTER 9

Taking It to Extremes

We may moan about being caught in a downpour, or marvel at an odd weather pattern but most of what we experience is perfectly normal. At the extreme ends of the weather spectrum, however, conditions range from the bizarre to the downright catastrophic.

LAHARS

Ash clouds and molten lava are the first deadly wave of a volcanic eruption, but there is another, equally lethal phenomenon which can be caused by the weather. A lahar is a mixture of ash, mud and rock mixed with water which flows down a river channel like a moving wall of wet concrete. Typically caused by heavy rainfall or a flood caused by melting ice, a lahar can flow at 35 kph (22 mph)

or more and up to 140 metres (460 ft) deep, destroying everything in its path. When it stops flowing, it sets like concrete, trapping vehicles, homes, animals and, tragically, people in its deadly grip.

In 1985, just such an event wiped out the town of Armero, in central Colombia. The initial eruption of the volcano Nevado del Ruiz melted the mountain's glaciers and sent four separate lahars pouring down its slopes at 60 kph (40mph), engulfing the town, where it killed more than 20,000 of its 29,000 inhabitants and 3,000 more in the surrounding villages.

The initial 1991 eruption of Mount Pinatubo in the Philippines claimed just six lives, but rains from a passing typhoon caused a devastating lahar. The mixture of ash, boulders and waters flowed into the heart of Angeles City, destroying bridges and buildings and killing 1,500 people.

In New Zealand, the government has installed a lahar warning system on Mount Ruapehu which proved its worth in 2007. A burst dam in a crater lake flooded the volcano and sent 1.4 million cubic metres of debris flowing down the Whangaehu river but the warning meant that roads, bridges and railways in the area had been closed and there were no fatalities.

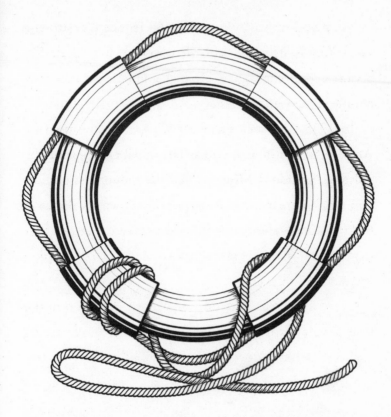

IT'S RAINING FISH AND FROGS

In May 2017, staff at Oroville elementary school in California thought they were being pranked when a scattering of fish and frogs appeared on the playground and rooftops after a shower of rain. But during the break, as children played outside, another fishy deluge pelted the pupils.

Bizarre as the report seems, the shower of fish and frogs was far from an isolated case. On 17 July 1841, a report in the *Atheneum* newspaper told of a fishy event in Derby, during a heavy thunderstorm:

> *Hundreds of small fish and frogs in great abundance descended with the torrents of rain. The fish were from half an inch to two inches long, and some considerably longer, one weighing three ounces. Many were picked up alive.*
>
> *The frogs were from the size of a horse bean to that of a garden bean. Numbers of them came down alive and jumped away as fast as they could but the bulk were killed by the fall onto the hard pavement.*

In New York, after a heavy shower in 1824, the streets were said to have been scattered with small fish and in 1931, a downpour of perch stopped the traffic in Bordeaux. After herring rained down in Scotland, in 1831, the mean-spirited landlords made tenants hand over their considerable bounty rather than making a meal of it, and in 1830, in Jelalpur, India, witnesses reported fish weighing up to six pounds dropping onto rooftops.

More recently, in 2004, Knighton, Powys, suffered a downpour of fish after a thunderstorm which baffled villagers, as they are some 50 miles from the coast. In the Indian province of Andhra Pradesh the phenomenon is relatively frequent – with three areas experiencing the falling fish in 2015 and 2016 alone. Other examples have been recorded in Australia, Canada, Sri Lanka, Nepal and many other counties.

Weird as it may seem, the explanation for the phenomenon is quite simple. During a storm strong updraughts are powerful enough to suck up small objects in their path. If they cross sea water or rivers, they are capable of picking up small fish, frogs and the like and carrying them several miles before dropping them. They can even be carried in the clouds as they are blown across the sky, only heading back down when the heavy rain starts.

WORM STOPS PLAY

In April 2011, a PE lesson at a school in Galashiels near Edinburgh was postponed when it started raining worms. Pupils were about to kick off a football match when they heard a 'soft thudding' on the ground and saw earthworms falling out of the sky.

Teacher David Crichton told *The Scotsman*: 'There were about 20 worms already on the ground at this point. Then they just kept coming down. The kids were laughing but some were covering their heads and others were running for cover for a while. They just scattered to get out of the way.' More were later found covering the nearby tennis courts.

Headmaster Kenny McKay added: 'None of the students were hurt, although they did find the experience quite bizarre. None of them will ever forget the day at school when worms fell out of the sky.'

A similar shower of creepy crawlies occurred in April 2015 in Norway, where biologist Karsten Erstad reported a light scattering on a snowy mountain where he was skiing. He counted 20 worms per square metre and concluded they could not have come from the ground, which was frozen under 15 metres (50 feet) of snow, so must have come from the sky. He said: 'When I found them on the snow they seemed to be dead, but when I put them in my hand I found that they were alive.'

As spring arrives, worms head for the surface of the earth. Worm showers can be caused by warm currents or thermals lifting them up as they emerge, and taking them some distance before the wind drops and they fall back onto the ground.

WET WEBBER

It sounds like an arachnophobe's nightmare, but the small Brazilian town of Santo Antonio di Platino suffered a downpour of spiders in February 2013. Captured on camera, the images soon went global, sending a shiver down many a spine as hundreds of the eight-legged creatures were seen descending towards the streets.

The bizarre event had come about because of a particular *species* of spider, *Anelosimus eximius*, which lives in colonies of thousands and spins a vast web in the canopies of trees in order to live and hunt together. On this occasion, a strong gust of wind is thought to have lifted the whole web and deposited it on the power lines above the town, and the confused critters were simply making their way back to earth by letting themselves down on silky threads.

FROZEN IN HORROR

Like something out of a black and white horror movie, homeowners in Minnesota stood by helplessly as houses were destroyed by a tsunami of ice in February 2013.

The unstoppable frozen wave poured out of Mille Lacs Lake, across roads into the homes, leaving a trail of destruction.

Homeowner Darla Johnson, who filmed the ice as it oozed across her lawn and uploaded the video, said: 'It was just pushing and breaking and pushing and breaking.' The ice covered about 4.8 km (3 miles) of shore, up to a height of 9 metres (30 feet) and destroyed or damaged 27 homes.

This rare event, known as an ice floe, is caused when a frozen lake begins to thaw and break up into small pieces and is then combined with strong winds which push the ice over the banks and onto land. In Minnesota, winds of 40 mph (65 kph) hit the lake and caused the overspill.

In the same week, another ice floe occurred in Manitoba, near Winnipeg in Canada when winds of 55 mph (88 kph) hit Dauphin Lake. Six homes were destroyed and fourteen others damaged.

Resident Dennis Stykalo, who lost his house, told the Canadian Broadcasting Company, 'You've got cement, concrete blocks and steel, and the ice goes through it like it's just a toothpick. It just shows the power. There is nothing you can do but just get out of the way and just watch.'

REINDEER MAGIC

Above the Arctic Circle, winter brings eleven weeks of total darkness, 24 hours a day. But for the reindeer that live there, that's not a problem because nature has provided them with a clever optical trick.

A small area of tissue behind the retina, the tapetum lucidum, changes with the seasons, from gold in the summer months to blue in winter. This allows the reindeer to pick up ultraviolet light and see in the dark.

They don't even need Rudolph to guide them on their way.

CRIMSON TIDE

Bondi Beach in Sydney is one of the most famous in the world but, on several occasions in the last few years, it has made the headlines for all the wrong reasons. In both 2012 and 2016, beachgoers were horrified when the sea turned bright red in a matter of minutes, with some fearing a shark attack.

In fact the crimson water was caused by a mass invasion of algae, encouraged by unusually warm weather. The sea temperature soared to 21°C from 17°C in a few days, causing an algae bloom, when the organisms gather together in the water. While the bloom is largely harmless, the resulting colour change is dramatic enough to cause swimmers to flee the waters in fear.

BLOOD RAIN

Blood-red rain, which stained clothes pink, fell for two months from July to September 2001 in the Indian province of Kerala. Mystified locals reported a huge bang, like a thunderclap, and a flash of light before the first colourful deluge on 25 July, and groves of trees were reported to have burnt shrivelled leaves.

Many believed the source of the rain was extraterrestrial, with the Centre for Earth Science Studies (CESS) blaming an exploding meteor which dispersed tiny particles into the atmosphere. Just a few days later, however, they retracted that theory after closer examination revealed the particles resembled spores, suggesting airborne algae had been picked up by the rain as it fell.

However, at first scientists were unable to locate any DNA and, while visitors to the region found a large amount of the rust-coloured lichen Trentepohlia growing on trees and buildings, they could not explain how so many spores could have become airborne at the same time. The lack of DNA led to the 'extraterrestrial origin' theory, formulated by scientists Godfrey Louis and Santhosh Kumar and backed by other leading academics.

Professor Chandra Wickramasinghe, Director of the Astrobiological Centre at Buckingham University, said: 'As far as the Kerala red rain is concerned, there is a mysterious microorganism that has defied identification so far. We have not been able to convincingly extract any DNA from them and Prof Louis has maintained that there is no DNA, but it can multiply at very high temperatures under high pressure conditions. I think there are all the signs of an alien bug! The Kerala red rain was preceded by a sonic boom that was heard, probably indicating that a fragment of a comet exploded in the atmosphere and unleashed the red cells that became incorporated in rain.'

However, further studies in November 2012, by Dr Rajkumar Gangappa and Dr Stuart Hogg from the University of Glamorgan, confirmed that the red rain cells did contain DNA. Three years later, a team of scientists from India and Austria studied the rain and reported that the colour was caused by the algal spores, *Trentepohlia annulata*, a species from Austria. They suggested that the spores had been transported to Kerala in clouds – a previously unheard of phenomenon.

Further instances of red rain have since occurred in India, in 2011, and in Sri Lanka, in 2012.

BALL LIGHTNING

As the villagers of Widecombe-in-the-Moor in Devon gathered at the Church of St Pancras on 21 October 1638, a severe storm was battering the Dartmoor region. Suddenly a ball of fire, measuring eight feet (2.4 metres) across, struck and entered the church, smashing pews and windows, sending stones from the walls crashing to the ground and filling the building with a thick, sulphurous smell.

Eyewitness reports claim the fireball then divided, with one part smashing a window as it burst out and another disappearing up the aisle. Four people were killed and sixty injured in the incident, which many blamed on a visit from the devil, due to the smell of burning sulphur. Others claimed it was the wrath of God blaming two unfortunate parishioners who were playing cards in the pew during the sermon.

In fact, what they had witnessed was ball lightning, an electrical phenomenon which occurs during a storm and lasts considerably longer than the usual flash of lightning, travelling at a slower speed but proving equally deadly. They are often seen to explode, scattering smaller balls in all directions.

In his 1875 book, French science writer Wilfrid de Fonvielle discussed 150 reported incidents of 'globular lightning' and observed: 'The motion of such balls is far from being very rapid – they have even been observed occasionally to pause in their course, but they are not the less destructive for all that. A ball of lightning which entered the church of Stralsund, on exploding, projected a number of balls which exploded in their turn like shells.'

Although these electrical spheres can be recreated in the lab, the unpredictable and fleeting nature of this natural phenomenon means it has evaded close study and not much is known about how it forms. But reports dating back centuries have recorded its devastating impact.

In 1726, a letter from John Howell described a 'large ball of fire' that hit the ship *Catherine and Mary* as it travelled through the Gulf of Florida. He wrote that the lightning 'split our mast in ten thousand pieces, if it were possible, split our main beam, also three planks of the side, under water, and three of the deck; killed one man, another had his hand carried off and had it not been for the violent rains, our sails would have been of a blast of fire.'

An 1809 account records three 'balls of fire' hitting the ship HMS *Warren Hastings* during a storm with the first killing a crew member, the second injuring a man who went to retrieve the body and a second fatality caused by ball number three.

One terrifying incident of ball lightning was witnessed by passengers on a flight from Washington to New York on 19 March 1963. Roger Clifton Jennison, Professor of Electronics at the University of Kent, was on the plane and observed: 'The aircraft encountered an electrical storm during which it was enveloped in a sudden bright and loud electrical discharge. Some seconds after this a glowing sphere a little more than 20 cm in diameter emerged from the pilot's cabin and passed down the aisle of the aircraft approximately 50 cm from me, maintaining the same height and course for the whole distance over which it could be observed.'

RUSSIAN ROULETTE

Tsar Nicholas II, the last Emperor of Russia, claimed he saw 'a fiery ball' at a small church in Alexandria where he and his grandfather, Tsar Alexander II, were attending an all-night vigil, when he was a boy:

During the service there was a powerful thunderstorm, streaks of lightning flashed one after the other, and it seemed as if the peals of thunder would shake even the church and the whole world to its foundations. Suddenly it became quite dark, a blast of wind from the open door blew out the flame of the candles which were lit in front of the iconostasis, there was a long clap of thunder, louder than before, and I suddenly saw a fiery ball flying from the window straight towards the head of the Emperor.

The ball (it was of lightning) whirled around the floor, then passed the chandelier and flew out through the door into the park. My heart froze, I glanced at my grandfather – his face was completely calm. He crossed himself just as calmly as he had when the fiery ball had flown near us, and I felt that it was unseemly and not courageous to be frightened as I was.

I felt that one had only to look at what was happening and believe in the mercy of God, as he, my grandfather, did. After the ball had passed through the whole church, and suddenly gone out through the door, I again looked at my grandfather. A faint smile was on his face, and he nodded his head at me. My panic disappeared, and from that time I had no more fear of storms.

HURRICANES

A hurricane is the most dangerous and destructive of storms, and can flatten buildings, trees and everything in its path.

To be classed as a hurricane, a storm front has to have low level winds of at least 74 mph circulating anti-clockwise in the northern hemisphere and clockwise in the southern hemisphere. The storm must be five to six miles high and at least 300 to 400 miles wide, although sometimes can be even bigger and it usually moves forward at speeds of 10–15 mph, although speeds of 40 mph have been recorded.

Hurricane, Tropical Cyclone or Typhoon?

The only difference between a hurricane, a tropical cyclone and a typhoon is where they are located. In the Atlantic and Northeast Pacific, it's a hurricane but the same storm in the Northwest Pacific is called a typhoon and in the South Pacific and Indian Ocean, it's a tropical cyclone.

The Strongest

The largest and most powerful typhoon in history hit the Philippines, China, Japan, Korea, Russia, Alaska and the

Caroline Islands in October 1979. Typhoon Tip, known in the Philippines as Typhoon Warling, reached a peak wind of 190 mph (305 kph) and measured 1,380 miles (2,220 km) in diameter.

The typhoon sank eight ships, with a loss of 44 fishermen, and indirectly caused a fire at Camp Fuji, a US military camp in Yokosuka, killing 13 Marines. Heavy rain brought by the storm in the mountains of Japan led to over 600 mudslides and flooded more than 22,000 homes. Throughout the country, 42 people died with another 71 missing and 283 injured and at least 11,000 people were left homeless.

The Deadliest

With winds of 140 mph (255 kph) the Bhola Cyclone, which hit the Bay of Bengal in November 1970, was not the strongest ever but it certainly took the most lives. A storm surge meant that the low-lying islands of the Ganges River delta in Pakistan were completely flooded. With no way to warn the islanders, most of whom were asleep when the floods hit on 12 November, everything was devastated and between 300,000 and 500,000 people perished.

The UK's Worst

Although the Great Storm of 1987 sticks in everyone's memory, it's not the worst storm the British Isles have seen.

On 26 November 1703, a devastating storm with winds up to 80 mph (128 kph) ripped across East Anglia, Northamptonshire and Suffolk, destroying villages as it went. Hundreds of ships and boats sank, Eddystone Lighthouse was swept away and between 8,000 and 15,000 people lost their lives.

Robinson Crusoe author Daniel Defoe later wrote a book called *The Storm* about the disaster, and it was published in 1704.

MAYAN MAYHEM

The word hurricane comes from the Huracan or Hurakan, the Mayan god of wind, storm and fire, also known as the Heart of Sky. He is one of four gods who helped create humanity, first with mud and water, which dissolved, and then with wood. But the carved wood figures, the manikins, angered the gods because they did not worship them so Hurakan sent a great flood to wreak destruction on Earth and then caused inanimate objects such as pans and stones to rise up and attack them until they were all dead.

Finally they made four men from a dough formed of corn and water, who proved so perfect that they were almost godlike themselves. The deities allowed them to live but clouded their vision to mar their perfection.

The name means 'one leg', and the volatile god was pictured with one human leg and one that looked like a serpent.

CHAPTER 10

Under the Weather: The Life of a Weather Presenter

Every time it's bad, I will get the blame OR get told that we 'didn't predict this' – which we probably did. I must also confess, though, that I do occasionally get praised for bringing nice weather too.

Simon King, weather presenter

Before heading out in the morning, most of us flick on the radio or breakfast TV to find out what the day has in store, and many of us will catch the forecast again throughout the day, or with the late night news. Our regular updates mean we know whether to take the brolly, cancel the picnic or just wear an extra layer of clothing before we step out of our front doors.

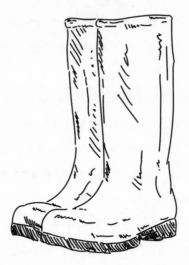

These reassuring bulletins are the job of a devoted group of weather presenters who work around the clock to keep us informed, braving the elements for outdoor broadcasts, risking technical meltdowns and hoping their predictions will prove spot on every day. But, just like the weather, things don't always go to plan.

'There are many things that have happened off screen such as equipment falling over or breaking, robotic cameras doing random things, fellow presenters falling off chairs or getting myself hopelessly tangled up in mic cable just seconds before going to air with a national forecast – all of which I've successfully covered up and hidden from those watching at home,' says presenter Matt Taylor. 'Sometimes things aren't so simple, though, and whilst you try to maintain your professionalism I was once defeated by a fly heading down my throat during a live broadcast on BBC Breakfast.

'I've also had a couple of occasions in the past where I've corpsed [started laughing uncontrollably] on air during Radio 2 forecasts on the Janice Long show – we both have the same sense of humour and it'd only take one of us to set the other off.'

Presenter Ben Rich has had similar moments in the BBC studios: 'Some of the funniest moments come when things go wrong – although they may not feel that funny at the time,' he admits. 'A classic was the time I started delivering my carefully crafted broadcast for the BBC News Channel … and was very quickly told through my earpiece that I wasn't wearing a microphone, and no one could hear me. The microphone in question was hanging up very close to me – but unfortunately tangled up with lots of other wires. Cue ten seconds of me untangling it, live on TV. Apparently that was quite funny, although I didn't enjoy it very much!'

But weather presenters aren't always kept in the warm, cosy studios to deliver their predictions to the nation. Producers seemed to relish seeing them, windswept or battered by rain, struggling to shout above the wind – and in some very odd places …

'I presented the weather on *Breakfast* for four years and on one occasion from Wicksteed Park in Kettering – while riding all the rollercoaster rides,' says Louise Lear.

Matt Taylor once delivered his forecast while 'waist deep in a pond full of cranberries' in the rain, and Darren Bett recalls one outside broadcast from a hill overlooking the football stadium in Huddersfield. 'The hill was so steep I had to stand on tiptoe so as not to fall over. My calf muscles were a lot stronger afterwards.'

But there is some glamour and excitement too. Carol Kirkwood is often up at the crack of dawn to report back from all corners of the country, and she's had some exhilarating experiences as a result. 'Some of the exciting things I have done "with weather" have included flying in a Red Arrow, jumping out of a plane with the Red Devils and attending Wimbledon and the Chelsea Flower Show every year,' she says. 'I love broadcasting from all around our glorious British countryside.'

Taking things outside can be fraught with danger, however.

'The funniest moments often tend to be on outside broadcasts,' admits Darren Bett. 'I once broadcast on a canal boat. Just before going on air I lost all sound and vision cues and at the same time, behind me, one barge crashed into another and the drivers were starting to fight. It reminded me of *Last of the Summer Wine*. I don't know how I stayed focused.'

ACTIVE SERVICE

I used to be a reserve officer in the Royal Air Force and was deployed to Camp Bastion in Afghanistan in 2010 to forecast the weather for the armed forces on operations there. Towards the end of my tour it happened to be National Science Week in the UK so in the lead up to it, BBC 5 Live thought it would be nice for me to broadcast from there to highlight why I'd been off air for so long and get me to talk about National Science Week.

As you might imagine, there were a lot of technical and security issues to get through to allow live broadcasts from a military operation. However, we overcame that and I broadcast live into 5 Live Breakfast one morning giving the UK's national weather forecast while sitting in the heat of Afghanistan – something I guarantee no one has done or will ever do again.

Simon King

FEELING SEASICK

BBC presenter Tomasz Schafernaker is a past master at the Shipping Forecast, but for one early morning broadcast he was clearly feeling under the weather.

Listeners to the 5.20 a.m. bulletin on 19 December 2016 were alarmed when the weatherman began spluttering on air before having to break off and run out of the room. It was the first time in the history of the Shipping Forecast that a presenter had failed to finish, but he had a very good excuse. Tomasz was suffering from a bout of sickness and had been trying not to vomit on air.

After rushing off from the studio, mid-Cromarty, he took to Twitter to explain. He wrote: 'Morning folks! Thanks for all the messages asking how I am this morning. Let me assure you that all is well. During the early morning shipping forecast I felt a bout of sickness coming on so I had to quickly jump ship and my colleague stepped in. Apologies for any distraction!'

SNOW JOKE

I used to broadcast live weather daily from the Blue Peter Garden at Television Centre. One particular year we had

quite a bit of snow, so BBC Breakfast decided to have some snow sculptors on the show, building something live on air. Throughout the programme, we followed the progress of the teapot that was being constructed – very appropriate when you think of the programme name.

Just before the final reveal, I checked if it was OK for me to touch the teapot in appreciation of the sculptors' hard work. They kindly said, 'Of course'. The studio presenters linked to me, and just before I got into the weather I tapped the teapot, saying what a magnificent job the sculptors had done. Then, to my horror, the whole structure collapsed, live on air. The sculptors' faces were priceless ... all their hard work ruined.

Meanwhile, I got a fit of the giggles, which was almost impossible to contain. I don't think they will ever come back!

Carol Kirkwood

STORMY WEATHER

Even the best weather forecasters are not infallible, as proved by respected meteorologist Michael Fish in a now infamous BBC broadcast on 15 October 1987.

Michael started his bulletin with the words: 'Earlier on today, apparently, a woman rang the BBC and said she heard there was a hurricane on the way ... Well, if you're watching, don't worry, there isn't!' He added that it would be 'very windy in Spain'.

Hours later, the Great Storm, with winds of up to 122 mph (194 kph) hit the UK claiming eighteen lives and felling over 15 million trees. Roads were blocked, buildings and railways damaged and hundreds of thousands were left without power, some for two weeks. The total bill for the damage caused came to over £1 billion.

Michael later revealed that the woman calling in to ask the question was a 'white lie' and that a member of staff at the BBC had said his mother was worried about a storm and he thought it would be a good opening line for his forecast.

Advances in technology mean that the 'Michael Fish moment', as it has since been dubbed, is unlikely to happen again.

'I've been presenting the weather for thirty years and I can honestly say we don't tend to get it drastically wrong,' says Louise Lear. 'Such a lot was learnt after the Great Storm of 1987. There are times when the rain or snow is a little faster or slower than anticipated and the problem is, because we're such a small island, that can be the difference between rain in the morning or the afternoon but when it comes to forecasting up to 48 hours, these days it's pretty accurate.'

RUNNING COMMENTARY

I once got a standing ovation from the team on the Danny Baker show on 5 Live after I breathlessly attempted to give a forecast. I'd been covering two shifts at once due to sickness, an extra broadcast that I'd picked up overran meaning that I had to sprint all the way from one side of TV Centre to the other in less than a minute.

I managed about twenty seconds of the forecast on his show before giving up.

Matt Taylor

I have a theory that once you've said the word 'snow' or 'thunder' people switch off and get into a flap about snow coming when you've actually warned them that there may be heavy snow forecast but only in the far north west of Scotland and at the very tops of the mountains.

Louise Lear

GETTING THE GIGGLES

My funniest moment was corpsing live on the News channel whilst presenting the weather with Simon McCoy.

In thirty years of broadcasting, I've never done that and certainly not for that long. I was in real danger of not being able to control myself, calm down and carry on. The News channel director was loving every minute of it and was determined to keep the camera on me for every second I was dying on air.

Fortunately it was great telly as it was obviously unplanned, and it became most watched clip of the day and the top story on the BBC News site.

Louise Lear

DON'T EAT THE YELLOW SNOW

A bitter spell of winter weather in 2014 caused the Met Office to issue a warning that caused much online hilarity. Forecasting the possibility of snow in Wales, they posted a 'yellow snow warning' – meaning 'be aware'.

But the article, posted under the headline 'Yellow snow warning for Wales', was shared by thousands and had many giggling over alternative meanings. One tweeted: 'When you've got to go, you've got to go,' and another added: 'PUBLIC TOILETS CLOSED? #YELLOW #SNOW #WARNING.'

The phrase 'yellow snow' is often used to describe snow which has been urinated on and featured in the

1974 Frank Zappa song 'Don't Eat The Yellow Snow', about a man who dreamt he was an Eskimo.

SPECIAL SKILLS

If weather is your passion then forecasting may be your dream job. So just what does it take to be a great weather presenter?

To become a forecaster at the Met Office a relevant degree – such as meteorology, physics, maths, environmental studies or geography – is necessary as well as a keen interest in weather. The training from there is provided in house.

The route into weather presenting is less clear cut, with some taking the traditional route and others coming to the job through other things. Helen Willetts and Tomasz Schafernaker, for example, took degrees in environmental studies and meteorology, respectively, before joining the Met Office and then the BBC. Louise Lear, on the other hand, studied Music and Arts and became a sports journalist before moving into weather. Carol Kirkwood was a businesswoman, working in recruitment, before becoming a freelance TV presenter and discovering her passion for the weather after her agent put her up for a job on the Weather Channel.

Whatever their way into the role, the presenters agree on the most important skill required to deliver a forecast.

'The biggest skill is the ability to ad-lib,' says Nick Miller. 'We don't have a script and can sometimes be required to ad-lib for up to four minutes. Also, we are doing this whilst hearing multiple voices from the gallery in our earpiece.

'This becomes extra difficult if you share the same first name as the news presenter. You're never sure when you hear your name whether the director is talking to you or the newsreader. Whatever happens, you must carry on talking.

'On one occasion, my weather graphics didn't appear on air properly and I had to talk for two minutes on the Six O'clock News with no maps to point to. I managed it, and when I finished no one in the studio had noticed that anything was amiss.'

Ben Rich agrees: 'We have to be able to ad-lib on live TV with no script, talking in time with the graphics, while the team in the gallery are talking loudly about something completely different through your earpiece. We have to be ready to adjust the duration of our forecast at any time if there's breaking news or a change to the programme running order. We also have to be able to talk knowledgeably about weather stories around the world – from floods to droughts, hurricanes to tornadoes.'

Another useful trait is the ability to pull a forecast out of your sleeve when you're spotted out and about.

'The general public are generally very kind and polite,' says Ben. 'But they always want to know what the weather's going to be like for their wedding/holiday/barbecue, even if it's weeks or months in the future.'

Being able to operate around the clock is also useful because, let's face it, the weather never sleeps.

'It's a 24/7 job and close to 20 years of waking up in the middle of the night, working into the early hours or doing nightshifts takes its toll sometimes,' says Matt Taylor. 'Trying to explain to your children why you are having to work at Christmas is never an easy one either.

'But being paid to enthuse about a subject you're passionate about is wonderful. As one of the main Breakfast weather presenters, I've also been incredibly lucky to have broadcast from a wide variety of stunning and unusual locations.'

Darren agrees the hours are sometimes a bit tough and jokes, 'It's only because I wear so much makeup that I don't look so tired.'

Ben adds: 'The best thing is the variety – every day is different and I get to talk about my passion for the weather all day long. The worst thing is the shifts – getting up at 3.45 a.m. for an early shift can be extremely painful!'

Generally the reaction from the public is very positive. Most people are quite shy – you can tell they've recognised you, but don't say anything. I was once followed around a department store by a woman who recognised my face and it turned out she thought I was a policeman.

Darren Bett

BOOZE NEWS

A Philadelphia forecaster livened up the weather map when a picture of his 'Wine forecast' went viral in March 2017.

Chris Sowers had actually been warning viewers of 6ABC about heavy snowfall that was expected in various regions, using a number of snow symbols to indicate the likely severity. But a mischievous fan doctored the image to show how much plonk people should stock up on for the coming blizzards. So the sign on Millville, for example read '3 bottles' and the more northern town of Reading was advised to stock up on '15 bottles.'

The image appeared on Chris's Twitter and was shared around the world, although he quickly clarified that the whole thing was a prank. He told *NY Magazine*: 'This is crazy. Just so everyone knows, this was Photoshopped. I didn't actually go on the air with a graphic like this. I can't believe how quickly this is spreading.'

FUNNY FRONT

Ad-libbing means that weather presenters can occasionally have a laugh on screen and BBC presenter John Hammond likes to crack a joke or two. In February 2013, he started one forecast with 'Good evening. Dull, grey, cold, miserable … and that's just me. The weather hasn't been great either.'

Channel 5 weather presenter Sian Welby became an internet sensation in 2015 with a forecast packed with *Star Wars* puns, including 'there's a Leia of cloud covering the UK', 'the Force is strong for northern Scotland' and 'tonight the weather strikes back'. In reference to Luke Skywalker, Darth Vader and Chewbacca, she told viewers: 'If you Luke father west you'll be seeing a glimmer of sunshine if you're Wookiee.' She then started making a habit of it, dropping movie puns into weather reports on numerous occasions, including a Batman vs Superman bulletin when she told viewers, 'Things have Gotham bad to worse,' and 'Cloud will be the Bane of the west.'

The worst thing about the job is having to tell people that the big event they've been planning for months will be a washout. Being right doesn't mean being happy about it!

Nick Miller

CHEEKY!

One year, when we hadn't had as much rainfall as we would have expected, I was demonstrating what we had and what we should have had, with measuring jugs and water.

In our headline sequence on BBC Breakfast, Bill Turnbull asked if I was going to be conducting my experiment again, to which I replied, 'Yes! I'll have my jugs out in 15 minutes.' That was years ago, and I am still scarred by it! Bill couldn't speak for laughing.

Carol Kirkwood

We have such a wonderful team of forecasters that we always give it our best shot to be as accurate as possible. But it's the British weather – it doesn't always play fair – and yes, things

don't always turn out as expected. You can never get too smug being a weather forecaster because there will only be one loser — the forecaster!

Nick Miller

BBC Books would like to thank Liz Howell, Director of BBC Weather and Liz Bentley, Chief Executive of the Royal Meteorological Society for their kind help and assistance with this book.